MODELS IN STRUCTURAL
INORGANIC CHEMISTRY

MODELS IN STRUCTURAL INORGANIC CHEMISTRY

A. F. WELLS

1970

OXFORD UNIVERSITY PRESS

NEW YORK AND OXFORD

Preface

SINCE most people experience difficulty in visualizing three-dimensional structures, models of various kinds are widely used in teaching. Organic chemistry is concerned largely with finite molecules or linear polymers formed from a small number of elements with relatively simple stereochemistries. Unless metal atoms are involved, models can be constructed from units that can be joined to two, three, or four others, provided that allowance is made for some variation in interbond angles.

The teaching of structural *inorganic* chemistry presents a quite different problem, for reasons that are discussed briefly in the introduction. It is difficult for the student to gain a real understanding of this subject from books or from lectures. Models for use in lecture rooms need to be inconveniently large and relatively simple if they are to be of value to the audience. Moreover, at a given time all the members of the audience see different views of a model and these are different from the view seen by the lecturer. There is no doubt that a far deeper insight into a structure is obtained if the student constructs the models with his (or her) own hands from simple structural units. The problem is therefore to design a course in model-building that is to form part of the *practical* work carried out by each student. This type of exercise should be introduced at the earliest possible stage in the teaching of chemistry, and many of the simpler models described in this book could well be built at school rather than at the university.

It is possible to build models of many molecules and crystal structures from drilled balls and spokes, even if all the balls are drilled with a standard set of holes. Nevertheless it is desirable to be able to construct models of various other types to emphasize particular features of structures such as, for example, the close-packing of the anions in a halide or oxide. Many structures are conveniently represented by using as building units the polyhedral coordination groups around the cations. The tetrahedron and octahedron are the most important coordination polyhedra because the cations in many halides and oxides occupy tetrahedral or octahedral holes between the close-packed anions. The use of these polyhedra to build three-dimensional models is analogous to the organic chemist's use of the hexagon as a shorthand symbol for a ring of six carbon atoms in a two-dimensional representation of a molecule. Since not all of the most suitable types of building units have hitherto been readily available the writing of a text and the provision of suitable building units have been regarded as aspects of the same problem.

The models to be described fall into five main groups: polyhedra, repeating patterns (2D and 3D nets), sphere packings, tetrahedral structures, and octahedral structures. In Part II of the book the intention has been to provide the student with the minimum amount of information thought to be necessary for the construction of a model, but where the instructions are inadequate, through accident or design, the notes and illustrations in Part III may be found helpful. It is important that the student should attempt the exercises and answer the questions *before* reading Part III. A number of exercises of a more advanced character are marked with an asterisk. Certain points in the introduction that may present difficulty are amplified in four appendices. For more detailed descriptions of molecular and crystal structures the reader is referred to the author's *Structural inorganic chemistry*, to which this book may be regarded as a 'practical' supplement.

This contribution to the teaching of inorganic chemistry is in itself very much of an experiment, and it is offered as a basis for development and adaptation in the light of experience. Needless to say, suggestions and comments from teachers and students would be much appreciated.

Acknowledgement

I wish to thank Dr. B. G. Bagley and the editor of *Nature* (*London*) for permission to reproduce Fig. 44.

                                                                    A. F. W.

Department of Chemistry and
Institute of Materials Science,
University of Connecticut
March 1969

Contents

CONTENTS   ix

Part I: Introduction

General Principles

CHEMICAL FORMULAE AND STRUCTURE

ELEMENTAL analysis of a compound consisting of discrete, finite molecules tells us the *relative* numbers of atoms of different elements, and this combined with a knowledge of the molecular weight gives the *actual* numbers of atoms that form a discrete group (molecule).

The structural problem consists of two parts.

(1) The *topology* of the molecule describes how the atoms are joined together, that is, which atoms are joined to which and by how many bonds.

(2) The *geometry* defines the relative positions of the atoms in space; it is concerned with bond lengths, interbond angles, and dihedral angles.

A knowledge of the geometry of a molecule obviously implies a knowledge of its topology, but until the development of physical methods such as spectroscopy and diffraction the chemist could, by experiment, study only the topology of molecules. In simple cases this follows directly from a knowledge of the combining powers of the atoms. For example, if there are to be four links from each C and one from each H atom, C_2H_2 can only be $H—C{\equiv}C—H$.

The topology of more complex molecules was deduced from the way in which they could be synthesized from or degraded into simpler units. It cannot be deduced from the chemical formula if there are alternative formulations satisfying the valences of the atoms (e.g. $CH_3CH_2CH_2CH_3$ or $HC(CH_3)_3$). These two forms of C_4H_{10} may be called *topological isomers* since they differ in the basic skeleton of connected carbon atoms in contrast to geometrical isomers such as the *cis* and *trans* forms of, for example, $aN{=}Na$, where a is an atom or group.

Only inspired guesses could be made about the *geometry* of molecules and then only about the local arrangements of bonds around certain atoms. The arrangements suggested usually corresponded to the most symmetrical ones; for example, four tetrahedral bonds from carbon and six octahedral bonds from cobalt (III). However, the less symmetrical square coplanar arrangement was proposed for four bonds from metals such as palladium and platinum. Supporting evidence for these stereochemistries came from studies of geometrical and optical isomerism.

It happened that the above guesses were correct and led, for example, to an elaborate structural chemistry of carbon compounds that has proved substantially correct in broad outline though necessarily lacking all precise geometrical details. This development of structural *organic* chemistry was possible because most organic compounds (other than polymers) exist as the same finite molecules in all states of aggregation. The structure of the molecule was usually deduced from its behaviour in solution, and the solid is simply an aggregate of molecules with essentially the same structure. No such development of structural *inorganic* chemistry was possible, for two main reasons. The first is that inorganic chemistry is concerned with approximately one hundred elements, many with much less symmetrical bond arrangements than those mentioned above. The second is that whereas reactions are usually carried out in solution (less frequently in the vapour state) most inorganic compounds are solids at ordinary temperatures.

THE IMPORTANCE OF THE SOLID STATE IN INORGANIC CHEMISTRY

While recognizing the importance of the gaseous and liquid states in the chemistry of the non-metallic elements, the following points should be emphasized.

(1) Most of the elements and the majority of simple inorganic compounds are solids at ordinary temperatures and usually over an appreciable range above room temperature.

(2) Relatively few simple inorganic compounds other than those of non-metals consist of finite molecules in the solid state. Instead, the atoms are bonded together into groups extending indefinitely in one, two, or three dimensions. These 'macro-molecules' must break down into finite groups (molecules or complex ions) or monatomic ions when the crystal is dissolved or vaporized, and therefore the atomic arrangement in the solid cannot be determined by normal chemical studies.

(3) Some large groups of inorganic compounds such as hydrates, 'acid' and 'basic' salts, and all non-stoichiometric compounds exist *only* in the solid state.

(4) Most elements and compounds are polymorphic. If there are two or more solid forms of a substance (element or compound) with different crystal structures, that is, different arrangements of the atoms, the substance is described as polymorphic. Some polymorphs correspond to different valence states of the atoms and have different numbers or arrangements of bonds from the atoms (e.g. diamond and graphite, grey and white tin). In other polymorphs the immediate environment of each kind of atom is the same, and polymorphs arise because there are alternative ways of linking the

atoms into, say, three-dimensional networks, as in the case of the two crystalline forms of ZnS. This type of polymorphism is the exact analogue of isomerism in a finite molecule. Far from being a topic of essentially crystallographic interest, polymorphism is an important and integral part of structural chemistry.

The formula of a *molecule* indicates the actual number of atoms forming a discrete group. However, the same type of formula is used for HCl, which consists of discrete molecules H—Cl in the solid, liquid, and gaseous states, and a salt such as NaCl, which exists in this form only in the vapour at high temperatures. At ordinary temperatures NaCl is a solid in which every ion is surrounded by six of the other kind. Only the first member of the series

AX	HI	AuI	CuI	NaI	CsI
Coordination number of A by X	1	2	4	6	8

exists as molecules. In all the other cases there is no direct relation between the formula and the structure of the (solid) compound because the crystals consist of repeating patterns of atoms in which the coordination number (c.n.) of A by X atoms (the number of X atoms surrounding an A atom) is greater than the ratio (one) of X to A atoms. Fig. 1 shows a number of arrangements, both finite and infinite, of equal numbers of A and X atoms.

In order to gain a real understanding of structural inorganic chemistry and hence to appreciate the relation between chemical formulae and the structures of molecules and crystals it is necessary to think in three rather than two dimensions and in terms of infinite as well as finite groups of atoms. For most people facility in 3-dimensional (3D) thinking is acquired only from the study of models. Moreover it is not sufficient merely to look at ready-made models. Far more insight into crystal structures is obtained by actually constructing models, and the models described in this book have been selected to illustrate the more important geometrical principles underlying the structures of inorganic compounds. Complementary to the practical study of models is an early introduction to patterns that repeat regularly in one, two, or three dimensions.

TWO APPROACHES TO INFINITE REPEATING PATTERNS

A cube may be described in two essentially different ways. It possesses numerous planes and axes of symmetry that necessarily pass through a point because a polyhedron is a finite object. This combination of symmetry elements (its point-group symmetry) is not peculiar to the cube; a regular octahedron, for example, has the same symmetry. However, if the orientation of one face in relation to the symmetry elements is defined, then the cube may

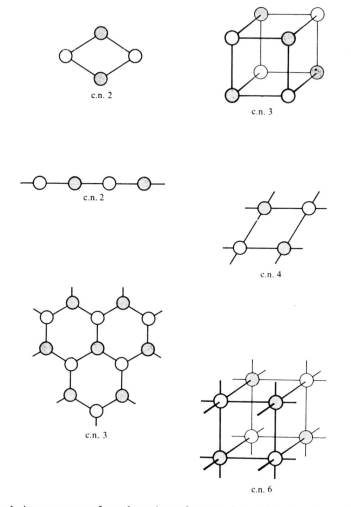

FIG. 1. Arrangements of equal numbers of atoms of two kinds (c.n. is coordination number).

be described as the object generated by this point-group. The symmetry ensures that the faces are regular polygons.

Alternatively, we may describe a cube as a system of 4-sided polygons so arranged that three edges meet at every point. From Euler's general relation between the numbers of vertices (N_0), edges (N_1), and faces (N_2) of a convex polyhedron: $N_0 + N_2 = N_1 + 2$, it can be shown (p. 156) that for a 3-connected polyhedron, that is, one in which three edges meet at every vertex,

$$3f_3 + 2f_4 + f_5 \pm 0f_6 - f_7 - 2f_8 - \ldots = 12,$$

where f_n is the number of n-gon faces. One of the (three) special solutions of this equation, namely, $f_4 = 6$, describes a polyhedron having six 4-sided faces and three edges meeting at each vertex. The above equation is concerned only with the way in which points and lines are connected to form polygons, and therefore the description $f_4 = 6$, $v_3 = 8$ (v_p being the number of vertices at which p edges meet) does not define a cube unless we also specify square faces.

Similarly, a repeating pattern may be derived by the operation of a set of symmetry elements combined with a lattice (1-, 2-, or 3-dimensional) or it may be built up by connecting points to specified numbers of others.

The historical development of these two approaches, which may be called the crystallographic and topological approaches, has been quite distinct. The first began in the latter part of the seventeenth century with the scientific study of the shapes of crystals and culminated in the derivation of the 230 space-groups (types of 3D symmetry) at the end of the last century. The topological approach to polyhedra and plane patterns dates from Euler's work in the middle of the eighteenth century; the Greek geometers of classical times appear to have had little interest in repeating patterns, though these were used in friezes and other surface decorations.

The topological approach is complementary to the conventional crystallographic one (via symmetry) and provides a unified treatment of connected systems of atoms in which discrete molecules and macromolecules are seen simply as end-members of the series

finite → 1-dimensional → 2-dimensional → 3-dimensional.

The basic idea is to recognize a structural unit, which may be a single atom or some convenient group of atoms (e.g. a tetrahedral SiO_4 group) and to show how these units are linked together to form the structure. Thus the diamond structure is first and foremost a 4-connected system or net. The possible structures that can be built from units that have to be bonded to four others are found by investigating 4-connected systems.

Owing to the very symmetrical arrangement of the four equal bonds from each carbon atom in diamond the structure has cubic symmetry. In crystallography it is conventional to describe a structure in terms of a unit cell, the edges of which are related to the symmetry elements (if any) of the structure. This unit cell is generally larger than the smallest one that could be chosen without reference to the symmetry. Thus the cubic unit cell of diamond contains eight atoms, but the structure may also be described in terms of a tetragonal cell containing four atoms or a triclinic cell containing two atoms. (For a note on crystal symmetry and unit cells see Appendix 4.) Moreover, a small distortion of a highly symmetrical structure such as diamond can reduce its symmetry and hence radically alter the crystallographic description of the structure, without altering its basic topology; that is, it remains essentially the same 3D network of 6-rings based on a repeat unit consisting of two atoms. Therefore, unless we are interested in the details of a structure, for example, the precise values of bond lengths or interbond angles, or the relation between symmetry and physical properties, the simpler topological description will be preferred to a crystallographic one.

The relevance of 4-connected systems to the structure of diamond is evident; it is less obvious that the structures of P_2O_5 are basically 3-connected systems. This oxide has three polymorphs, one of which consists of P_4O_{10} molecules.

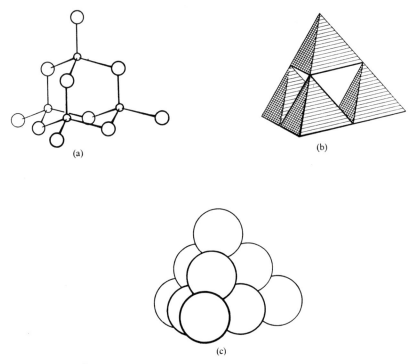

(a)

(b)

(c)

FIG. 2. Three representations of the P_4O_{10} molecule.

This molecule may be visualized in three ways (Fig. 2): (a) as an assembly of P atoms, each forming four bonds, and O atoms, six of which are bonded to two P atoms and four to one P atom; (b) as four tetrahedral PO_4 groups, each of which shares three vertices (O atoms) with other similar groups; (c) as an approximately close-packed assembly of ten O atoms in which P atoms occupy positions of tetrahedral coordination. Because the other two forms of crystalline phosphorus pentoxide are based on the same structural principle, namely, the sharing of three vertices by each PO_4 group, the problem is reduced to a study of 3-connected systems. The structural chemistry of this oxide can in fact be described in this very simple way.

The representation of Fig. 2(c) is less abstract than (a) or (b) in that it shows the large oxygen atoms as responsible for the volume of the molecule. These three models suggest that the study of molecular and crystal models can conveniently be based on three main types of constructional unit: drilled balls and spokes, polyhedra, particularly tetrahedra and octahedra, and balls for constructing closest packings and other types of sphere packing. In many crystals the largest atoms are those of oxygen, sulphur, or halogens, and their structures may be described in terms of the packing of these atoms. A study of the packing of spheres is therefore complementary to the study of structures of low coordination by ball-and-spoke models.

The construction of the three P_4O_{10} molecules of Fig. 2 forms an excellent introduction to a practical course of the type outlined in this book.

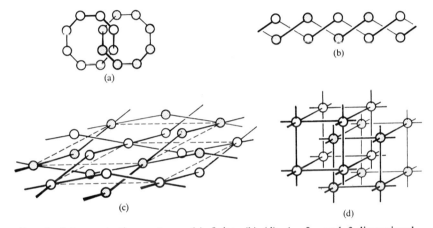

FIG. 3. Interpenetrating systems: (a) finite, (b)–(d), 1-, 2-, and 3-dimensional.

The topological approach is most suited to the description of structures in which the atoms (or other units) are linked to a relatively small number of others (three to six). This, however, is not a serious limitation because the relatively few important structures of higher connectedness (coordination number) are easily added. Moreover, the structures of many quite complex compounds are based on simple 3-, 4-, or 6-connected systems, the structural unit that is linked to three, four, or six others being itself a complex grouping of atoms. The great advantage of a topological treatment is that it emphasizes the basic features of a structure by describing it initially in the simplest possible way, and it shows how a small number of very simple structural themes are utilized in crystalline compounds of many different chemical types. Furthermore, we shall find that some points relating to the structures of crystalline compounds are not in fact matters of crystal chemistry at all but instead involve only simple topological considerations. For example, no compounds A_2X_3 (for example, sesquioxides or sesquisulphides) crystallize with simple layer structures in which the coordination numbers of A and X are 6 and 4 respectively because it is impossible to construct the appropriate plane net; this point is discussed in Appendix 2.

We have supposed that in any system all the points together form one connected net, that is, it is possible to travel along links from any point to any other. There are some very interesting structures in which this is not possible, namely, those consisting of two or more interpenetrating (interlocking) structures (Fig. 3). The simplest of these is a pair of linked n-rings, isomeric with a single $2n$-ring. It is likely that some molecules of this kind are formed in many ring-closure reactions in which large rings are formed. No examples of intertwined linear systems are known in the inorganic field, but an interesting example of two 'interwoven' layers is found in crystalline silver tricyanomethide, $Ag[C(CN)_3]$. Several examples are now known of crystals built of two or more identical interpenetrating 3D nets, some of which will be mentioned in connection with the diamond structure.

THE BASIC SYSTEMS OF CONNECTED POINTS

However complex the units that are to be joined together, the problem may be reduced to the derivation of systems of points each of which is connected to some number (p) of others. In the simplest systems this number is the same for all points:

$p = 1$: there is one solution only, a pair of connected points.

$p = 2$: the only possibilities are closed rings or an infinite chain.

$p \geqslant 3$: the possible systems now include finite groups (for example, polyhedra) and arrangements extending indefinitely in one, two, or three dimensions (p-connected nets).

It is not necessary to include singly connected points ($p = 1$) in nets since they can play no part in extending the net. Also, 2-connected points may be added along the links of any more highly connected net ($p > 2$) without altering the basic system of connected points. We therefore do not include either 1- or 2-connected points when deriving the basic nets though it may be necessary to add them to obtain the structures of actual compounds from the basic nets. For example, 2-connected points (representing —O— atoms) are added along the edges of the 3-connected tetrahedral group of four P atoms to form the P_4O_6 molecule, and additional singly connected points (representing O= atoms) at the vertices to form P_4O_{10}.

Still retaining the condition that all points have the same connectedness, we find that there are certain limitations on the types of system that can be formed. For example, there are no polyhedra with all vertices 6-connected, and there is only one 6-connected plane net. These limitations are summarized in Table 1, which may be considered in two ways.

(i) Together with simple linear systems ($p = 2$) the *vertical* subdivisions correspond to the four main classes of crystal structure, namely, molecular crystals, chain, layer, and 3-dimensional (macromolecular) structures. The division into polyhedra, plane, and 3D nets is also the logical one for the systematic derivation of these systems.

(ii) However, from the chemical standpoint we are more interested in the *horizontal* sections of Table 1. If we wish to discuss the structures that are possible for a particular type of unit, for example, an atom or group that is to be bonded to three others, we have to select from the vertical groups the systems having $p = 3$.

TABLE 1. *Systems of p-connected points*

p	Polyhedra	Infinite periodic nets	
		Plane nets	3D nets
3			
4			
5			
6		(one only)	
7			

For our present purpose it is sufficient to summarize here some of the simpler 3- and 4-connected systems and to give examples of structures based on three of them. For a more systematic treatment of polyhedra, plane, and 3D nets the reader is referred to the appendices.

3-connected systems

These include three of the regular solids (tetrahedron, cube, and pentagonal dodecahedron), a number of semi-regular solids, notably the truncated tetrahedron, truncated octahedron, and the prisms, linear systems, plane, and 3D nets. Those of most interest in structural chemistry are illustrated in Fig. 4. Some of the numerous structures based on the plane 6-gon net are mentioned later. The other two plane nets shown in Fig. 4 represent diagrammatically the layers in certain minerals formed from tetrahedral SiO_4 or AlO_4 groups which share three of their vertices (O atoms).

As yet there is only one example of the 3D net (d). In crystalline hydrogen peroxide each molecule is hydrogen-bonded to four others, and the crystal may therefore be represented as a 3D framework in which one-third of the

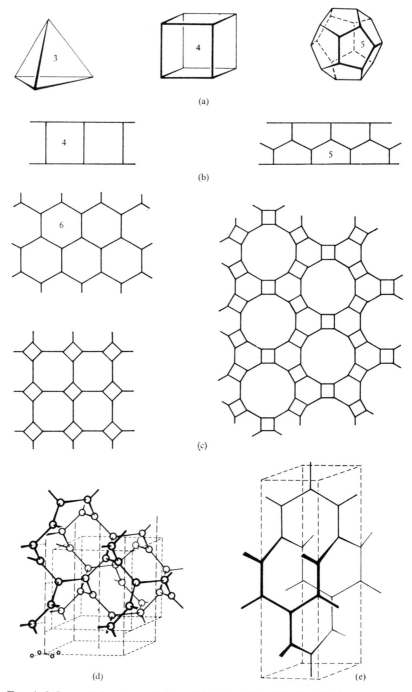

FIG. 4. 3-Connected systems, finite and infinite: (a) polyhedra, (b) linear systems, (c) plane nets, (d) 3D nets.

links are O—O bonds of H_2O_2 molecules and the remainder O—H···O bridges. The net (e) represents the arrangement of 3-connected silicon atoms in $ThSi_2$ and, rather more diagrammatically, the structure of one of the polymorphs of P_2O_5. As already noted, the crystalline forms of this oxide illustrate three ways of linking together PO_4 tetrahedra by sharing three vertices with other similar groups.

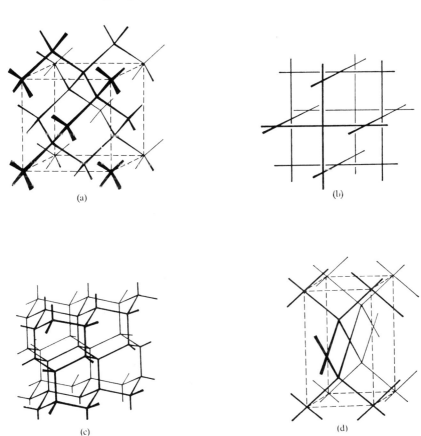

(a)

(b)

(c)

(d)

FIG. 5. Some 3-dimensional 4-connected nets (see text).

4-connected systems

Of the polyhedra in this group there is only one regular solid, the octahedron; semi-regular solids include the cuboctahedron and the antiprisms. Of the plane 4-connected nets we need note only the simplest, the quadrilateral (square) net, but a number of 3D nets are important. The nets (a) and (b) of Fig. 5 are suited to units forming four tetrahedral or four coplanar bonds

respectively. The only known example of the net (b) is the remarkable
structure of NbO, alternate atoms being Nb and O, but examples of structures
based on the net (a) are numerous, and some are described later. In its most
symmetrical form this net represents the structure of diamond, cubic ZnS,
and the cubic forms of H_2O and SiO_2 (cristobalite). There is an indefinitely
large number of more complex 4-connected nets, including nets suitable for
atoms forming tetrahedral bonds (for example, (c)) and others in which some

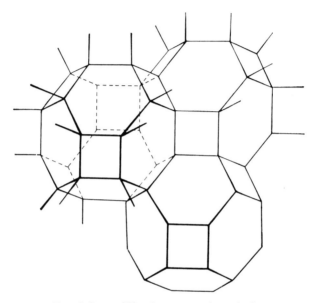

FIG. 6. Space-filling by truncated octahedra.

points have four tetrahedral and others four coplanar neighbours (as in
PtS, (d)) and a particularly interesting group in which the links enclose
polyhedral cavities.

For this to be possible at least four links must meet at each point. The
simplest nets of this type were derived by Fedorov (1895) and Andreini (1907)
who were interested in space-filling arrangements of polyhedra. In such
arrangements the edges of the polyhedra form a 3D net, and in the more
symmetrical ones the same number of edges meet at each point (vertex). The
packing of truncated octahedra (Fig. 6) is of interest not only in connection
with the cellular structure of foams and the arrangement of the crystal grains
in polycrystalline metals but also as the basic framework underlying the
atomic structures of ultramarine ($Na_8Al_6Si_6O_{24}S_2$) and $HPF_6.6H_2O$. In the
former crystal the points represent the centres of SiO_4 or AlO_4 tetrahedra
which share all vertices to form a 3D framework which accommodates the

Na^+ and S_2^{2-} ions, while in $HPF_6.6H_2O$ the net represents the hydrogen-bonded framework of water molecules, each linked to its four neighbours by $O—H\cdots O$ bridges. Other examples of crystals based on polyhedral frame-

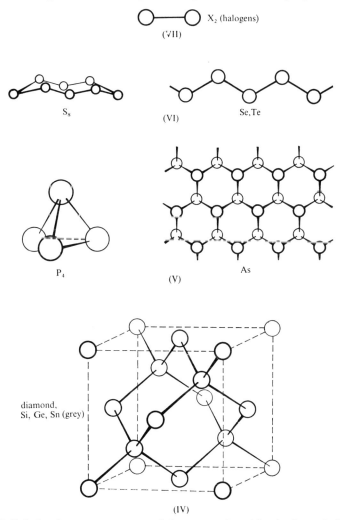

FIG. 7. Relation between structures of elements and position in the periodic table.

works include clathrate hydrates, such as $Cl_2.7\frac{2}{3}H_2O$ and $Br_2.8\cdot6H_2O$, and zeolites (4-connected), and the boron skeletons in CaB_6 and UB_{12} (5-connected).

To illustrate the topological approach to the structures of inorganic compounds we now show how some of the simpler types of connected system are utilized in molecules and crystals.

THE '8−N' RULE

The structures of the elements Cl, S, P, and Si (Fig. 7) provide the simplest example of the relation between bond-forming capacity (or electronic structure) and atomic arrangement. The number of bonds formed is $8 - N$, where N is the ordinal number of the periodic group, e.g. 4 for C and Si, 5 for N and P.

$p = 1$: Cl–Cl molecule in all states of aggregation.

$p = 2$: cyclic S_6 and S_8 molecules in different crystalline forms and in the vapours from them, and infinite chains in plastic sulphur.

$p = 3$: tetrahedral P_4 molecule, 3-connected (puckered) 6-gon layer in black phosphorus.

$p = 4$: diamond-like structure of elementary silicon.

The same principles determine the structures of the oxides and oxy-ions of these elements in their highest oxidation states, the structural unit being a tetrahedral MO_4 group:

p	Oxy-ion			Oxide molecule
1	pyro	$Si_2O_7^{6-}$	$P_2O_7^{4-}$	$S_2O_7^{2-}$	Cl_2O, finite
2	meta	$(SiO_3)_n^{2n-}$	$(PO_3)_n^{n-}$	$(SO_3)_n$	cyclic or linear
3	infinite 2D	$(Si_2O_5)_n^{2n-}$	$(P_2O_5)_n$		polyhedral, 2 D, or 3D
4		$(SiO_2)_n$			infinite 3D

THE PLANE HEXAGONAL NET

Some structural units that can be linked together to form this, the simplest 3-connected plane net, are illustrated in Fig. 8. The single atom (a) can be directly linked or linked through atoms or groups of a second kind to give a layer of composition A_2X_3 (b). Tetrahedral AX_4 groups (c) sharing three vertices form a layer of composition A_2X_5, and octahedral groups AX_6 sharing three edges form a layer AX_3 (d). The unit (e) represents a hydrogen-bonded molecule of a dihydroxy compound HO.R.OH. Crystalline hydrogen peroxide has already been mentioned as forming a 3-dimensional 3-connected net. Examples include

(a) graphite, AlB_2, and BN, in all of which the net is strictly planar; As and $CaSi_2$, in which it is buckled; and black P, in which the buckling is still more marked owing to reduction of the interbond angle from 120° (plane net) to approximately 100°;

(b) As_2O_3 (monoclinic form) and As_2S_3 (orpiment);

(c) neutral P_2O_5 layer in one polymorph of phosphorus pentoxide, 2-dimensional ion in $Li_2Si_2O_5$;

(d) $AlCl_3$, $CrCl_3$, $Al(OH)_3$;

(e) γ-quinol (HO.C_6H_4.OH).

Hexagonal sheets of linked SiO_4 or AlO_4 tetrahedra, (c), are components of the more complex layers in micas, talc, kaolin, and other clay minerals. We referred earlier to silver tricyanomethide as an example of a crystal consisting of two 'interwoven' hexagonal nets.

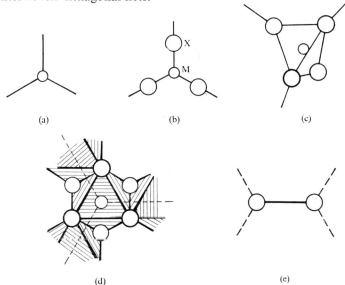

FIG. 8. Some 3-connected units.

THE SQUARE PLANAR NET

Atomic arrangements based on this, the simplest 4-connected plane net, can be classified in a similar way to those of the previous paragraph, the structural units being 4-connected ones (Fig. 9).

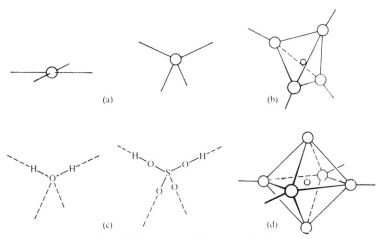

FIG. 9. Examples of 4-connected units.

(a) The red form of PbO is built of layers within which Pb and O atoms alternate, the coplanar O atoms forming tetrahedral bonds to Pb atoms lying on either side of the O layer. LiOH has a similar structure, Li replacing O and OH replacing Pb.

(b) and (c) Both correspond to the composition AX_2 as in red HgI_2, which is built of tetrahedral HgI_4 groups sharing all vertices. More complex examples of this general type include $CuCN.N_2H_4$, in which both CN and N_2H_4 act as bridging ligands, and crystalline sulphuric acid, which consists of layers of hydrogen-bonded $O_2S(OH)_2$ molecules forming the plane 4-gon net.

(d) Simple examples of octahedral AX_6 groups sharing four equatorial X atoms are the infinite 2D molecule of SnF_4 and the $(NiF_4)_n^{2n-}$ layer in K_2NiF_4 and the similar layers in numerous complex fluorides and oxides with this structure. In $UO_2(OH)_2$, originally formulated $UO_3.H_2O$, octahedral units $UO_2(OH)_4$ share the equatorial OH groups to form the same kind of layer.

THE DIAMOND NET

The simplest 3-dimensional 4-connected framework provides an excellent illustration of the way in which one basic pattern serves for the structures of a large number of crystals of very different chemical types. It is not proposed to comment on all the structures of Table 2, but attention should perhaps be drawn to those which consist of two or more interpenetrating nets. The first structure of this kind to be determined was the cuprite (Cu_2O) structure. Oxygen atoms at the points of the diamond net are linked through Cu atoms, and the crystal consists of two identical interpenetrating 3-dimensional nets which are not cross-connected by any primary Cu—O bonds. The structures of the borates listed at the right-hand side of Table 2 are described on p. 45. The most complex structure of this type so far discovered is that of $Cu[NC(CH_2)_4CN]_2NO_3$, in which the cation consists of six interpenetrating frameworks, each formed from Cu(I) atoms placed at the points of a diamond net and linked through adiponitrile molecules, $NC(CH_2)_4CN$.

TABLE 2. *Structures based on the diamond net*

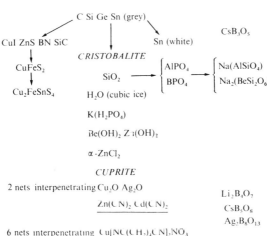

These examples should suffice to show that some relatively simple inorganic compounds have a very interesting structural chemistry. By grouping structures according to the basic topological pattern we not only simplify the description of the structures but also illustrate the very economical use in nature of a minimum number of simple and elegant structural patterns.

NON-PERIODIC STRUCTURES

The amount and type of information obtainable by diffraction studies (X-ray, electron, or neutron) depend largely on the extent to which a system approximates to a regular diffraction grating. Crystallographers are therefore usually interested in atomic arrangements that repeat regularly in three (less frequently two or one) dimensions. 'Normal' crystalline solids depart from perfect 3-dimensional periodicity in a number of ways, for example, in having small numbers of atoms missing or misplaced. In solid solutions there is random arrangement of atoms of two or more kinds in sites which are equivalent as far as the symmetry of the structure is concerned, so that although the *pattern* of sites occupied is regular the whole structure is not periodic if account is taken of the nature of the atoms.

There is another quite different type of non-periodic structure about which little is known because there seems to be no physical means of proving its existence, but which may nevertheless be important in some solid (or super-cooled liquid) phases. Ordering might start at a point and lead to some kind of structure which, although regulated by definite 'rules', cannot extend indefinitely for purely topological or geometrical reasons. For example, in a covalent system or in a glass a system of 5-rings might form that is not part of any possible 3-dimensional net. Sphere packings can be envisaged that are not periodic in three dimensions. If there is a simple mechanism for conversion to a more dense packing, as in the case of the icosahedral packing described on p. 54, the non-periodic packing is unlikely to persist. In the absence of such an alternative structure, however, the non-periodic structure might exist indefinitely. Systems radiating from a point or from a unique axis may well be of interest in some structural problems. We shall therefore include examples of such systems, although by far the greater number of models to be described represent portions of periodic 3-dimensional structures characteristic of normal crystalline solids.

Units for Construction of Models

THE models described in this book are built from the following types of unit.

(1) Plastic connectors and rod (tube). For the models of polyhedra the minimum requirements are:

        12 5-connectors and 12 6-connectors,
        24 lengths of rod (blue), 65 mm ($2\frac{1}{2}$ in approx.),
        30 lengths of rod (red), 75 mm (3 in approx.).
        6 lengths of rod (yellow), 75 mm (3 in approx.),

(2) Drilled balls and spokes. The 26 holes drilled in each ball correspond to the axial symmetry of the cube (Fig. 10), namely:

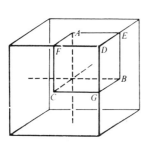 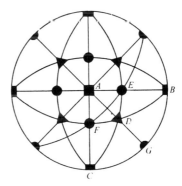

FIG. 10. Relation between cube and the 26-hole ball.

    3 axes of 4-fold symmetry (6 holes of type A, B, C),
    4 axes of 3-fold symmetry (8 holes of type D),
    6 axes of 2-fold symmetry (12 holes of type E, F, G).

It follows that $AE = CG = 45°$; $GE = 60°$; $AD = 55°$ (approx.). Check which combinations of holes give angles of $109\frac{1}{2}°$, $120°$, $135°$, and $150°$. The models require 40 balls, 20 each of two colours, and 100 spokes.

(3) Transparent and coloured hollow plastic spheres (unit radius) for close-packing models and smaller coloured (solid) spheres with radii 0·225 and 0·414 units, which fit into the tetrahedral and octahedral interstices. One sphere of radius 0·732 units is used in one model.

For building many of the models it is convenient to have spheres permanently joined to form (a) portions of c.p. layers, (b) portions of c.p. XO_3

layers, and (c) groups of spheres (Fig. 11). Coloured spheres are used for the shaded circles in Fig. 11(b) and (c). Numbers of units required are

        c.p. X layers (a), 4; c.p. XO_3 layers (b), 4;

        3-sphere units, 4;

        6-sphere units, 5;

        7-sphere units, 1;

        pentagonal units, 1;

        spheres for tetrahedral holes, 20;

        spheres for octahedral holes, 10 each of two colours.

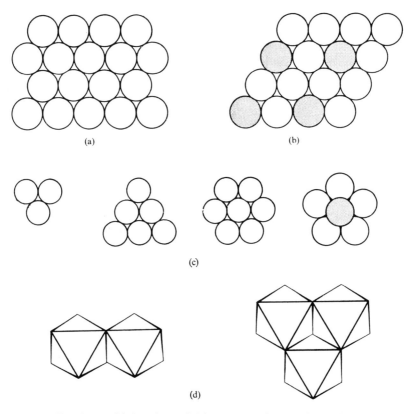

FIG. 11. Multiple units useful for constructing certain models.

(4) Tetrahedra and octahedra (with holes at their vertices) which can be joined together by flexible connectors to share vertices, edges, or faces. Certain models can be more easily constructed from multiple units consisting of two or three octahedra joined at certain edges as shown in Fig. 11(d).

Requirements are

	connectors
single tetrahedra, 50;	2-linear, 50;
single octahedra, 26;	3-planar, 25;
2-octahedra units, 6;	4-planar, 25;
3-octahedra units, 4.	

The 4-planar connectors may be used as (linear) 2-connectors, as 3-connectors, or as 4-tetrahedral connectors. Objects that will serve as tri-capped trigonal prisms (12) may be made from three half-octahedra (36).

Part II: Model-building

1. Polyhedra and other Finite Systems

WE HAVE seen in the introduction that some knowledge of polyhedra is essential to an understanding of structural chemistry. A general introduction to polyhedra in Appendix 1 includes information about the regular and semi-regular bodies and certain others that are of interest in connection with the structures of crystals.

The atoms surrounding the central atom in a finite complex ion or coordination compound or the nearest neighbours of an atom in a crystal form a polyhedral coordination group. Some coordination groups are highly symmetrical, as, for example, a regular octahedral group, but there is often a less regular arrangement of nearest neighbours, particularly if these are atoms of different elements. In such cases the description of the coordination polyhedron is difficult, and in this connection the relations between certain pairs of polyhedra (with the same number of vertices) are relevant. A 4-gon face can be buckled to form two triangular faces, so that a cube ($f_4 = 6$) is converted in this way into the square antiprism ($f_4 = 2, f_3 = 8$) and then to the triangulated dodecahedron ($f_3 = 12$). We shall study the following pairs of polyhedra which are related in this way:

Number of vertices	Triangular faces only	Square and triangular faces
5	Trigonal bipyramid	Tetragonal pyramid
6	Octahedron	Trigonal prism
8	Bisdisphenoid	Square antiprism
9	Tricapped trigonal prism	Monocapped anti-prism
12	Icosahedron	Cuboctahedron

In some crystals the distances from an atom to the surrounding ones cover a considerable range and it is difficult to decide which atoms should be counted as 'nearest neighbours'. In the absence of well-defined groups of approximately equidistant nearest neighbours the structure may be described in terms of the polyhedral *domains* of the atoms. Planes are drawn perpendicular to and passing through the mid-points of lines connecting each atom to its neighbours. These planes enclose polyhedra around each atom, and the structure is described as a space-filling assembly of polyhedral domains of various kinds. Space-filling assemblies of polyhedra are also of interest in another connection, namely, that the edges of the polyhedra form a 3-dimensional framework. A model of one framework of this kind will be described under 3D nets.

SYSTEMS OF CONNECTED POINTS

P.1. Find the simplest arrangements of points in which each point is joined to (a) three and (b) four others. Use rods, all of the same length, and connectors.

P.2. Find the systems in which respectively 3, 4, 5, and 6 equilateral triangles meet at each point.

P.3. Find the systems in which respectively 3, 4, 5, and 6 squares meet at each point.

4-coordination

P.4. *Tetrahedron*

Draw sketches of a regular tetrahedron viewed (a) perpendicular to a face, and (b) along a line joining mid-points of opposite edges.

Calculate the (maximum) distance between centres of two regular tetrahedra (edge length l) sharing a vertex, edge, or face.

5-coordination

***P.5.** *Tetragonal pyramid and trigonal bipyramid*

With eight rods of equal length construct a half-octahedron (square pyramid). An atom placed at the centre of the base is equidistant from the five vertices. Now insert a ninth rod, of the same length as the other eight, as one diagonal of the base. The figure becomes a trigonal bipyramid.

6-coordination

P.6. *Octahedron and trigonal prism*

Construct an octahedron using 5-connectors and plastic rods of a different colour for the three edges emphasized in Fig. 12(a) and leaving spare connectors projecting into the face *ABC*. Make a second octahedron which is the mirror image of the first, and check that it is not possible to bring one into coincidence with the other, i.e. that an octahedron with these three edges distinguished from the others is enantiomorphic.

Now remove these three edges from one octahedron (the broken lines in Fig. 12(b)). The polyhedron produced is a *trigonal prism*.

An octahedron is usually illustrated as in Fig. 12(c), referred to the conventional orthogonal axes. An octahedral object is not likely to be encountered in this orientation, and in illustrations of crystal structures it is often viewed in other directions. It is therefore important that such projections are recognizable.

Sketch an octahedron viewed along a line joining
(a) opposite vertices,
(b) the mid-points of opposite edges,
(c) the mid-points of opposite faces.
(d) How many isomers are there of octahedral complexes AX_4Y_2 and

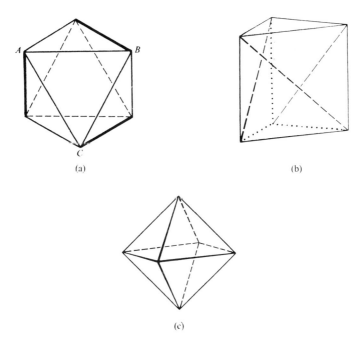

(a)

(b)

(c)

FIG. 12. Octahedron and trigonal prism.

AX_3Y_3, and (e) what are the corresponding numbers if the ligands are arranged at the vertices of a trigonal prism?

(f) How many isomers are there of an octahedral complex AX_2D_2, where D is a chelate ligand, i.e. one occupying two (*cis*) bond positions (e.g. $C_2O_4^{2-}$ or $H_2N.CH_2CH_2.NH_2$)?

Calculate the maximum distance between the centres of two octahedra of edge length l sharing (g) one vertex, (h) one edge, or (i) one face.

For examples of molecules or complex ions in which two octahedral groups share a vertex, edge, or face, see p. 87.

7-coordination

*P.7. Add a cap to the first octahedron using the remaining connectors pointing into the face ABC of Fig. 12(a). The mono-capped octahedron, with one triangular face enlarged and the seventh atom brought nearer to the centre of the face, is the coordination polyhedron around the metal ion in the A (high-temperature) form of La_2O_3 and numerous $4f$ and $5f$ sesquioxides.

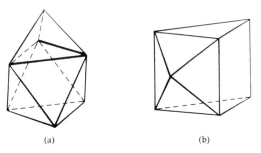

(a)   (b)

FIG. 13. Mono-capped octahedron and trigonal prism.

Removal of the two edges emphasized in Fig. 13(a) from the mono-capped octahedron leaves a mono-capped trigonal prism (Fig. 13(b)). The anions in K_2NbF_7 and K_2TaF_7 have this structure, whereas those in K_3UF_7 and K_3ZrF_7 have a pentagonal bipyramidal shape. The structure of crystalline $PaCl_5$ provides an example of an infinite linear molecule consisting of pentagonal bipyramidal groups sharing two (non-adjacent) edges.

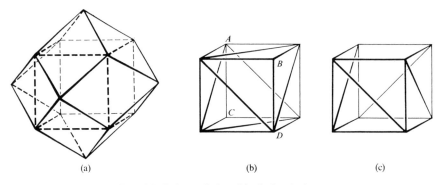

(a)   (b)   (c)

FIG. 14. Cube and rhombic dodecahedron.

8-coordination

P.8. *Cube and rhombohedron*

Construct a cube from rods and 6-connectors leaving four unused connectors pointing into each face.

Draw a sketch of the cube viewed along a body-diagonal. Compression or extension along one body-diagonal converts a cube into a *rhombohedron*.

What parameters must be specified to define a rhombohedron?

Add a square pyramid above each face of the cube using the shorter rods (of length $\frac{1}{2}\sqrt{3}$). The polyhedron formed is the rhombic dodecahedron (Fig. 14(a)). What figure do the added vertices outline?

To a cube add the face-diagonals shown in Fig. 14(b), using rods of the same length as the cube edges. The object formed is a 'compound' polyhedron, being built of an octahedron sharing opposite faces with two regular tetrahedra. The 'bi-capped octahedron' in this form is clearly not a possible coordination polyhedron in crystals because two vertices are at a very large distance from the centre of the octahedron.

What figure would be formed if the diagonals of the vertical faces are inserted as in Fig. 14(b) but the diagonals AB and CD are inserted instead of those shown? It should be possible to answer this question without making a model, by considering the numbers of connections to the vertices A and D. Why could this polyhedron not be constructed from eighteen rods of equal length?

Insert the face-diagonals shown in Fig. 14(c) using rods of the same length as the edges of the cube. What is the name of this polyhedron?

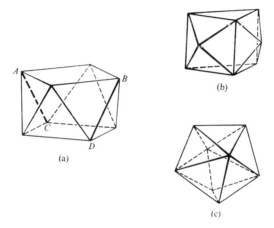

FIG. 15. Square antiprism and bisdisphenoid.

P.9. *Square antiprism and bisdisphenoid*

Construct a square antiprism with 3-in. rods and 5-connectors leaving the spare connectors pointing towards the centres of the square faces and using sticks of a different colour (e.g. yellow) for the two edges AC and BD (Fig. 15(a)). Add a third yellow stick as the diagonal AB of a square face, and orient the model with the other square face and the third yellow stick vertical. It is now a *bi-capped trigonal prism* (Fig. 15(b)).

Now add the diagonal CD of the other square face (yellow stick). The figure is a *bisdisphenoid* (Fig. 15(c)), so-called because it consists of two interpenetrating disphenoids, the latter being a general term for a tetrahedron. The yellow sticks connect the vertices of a flattened tetrahedron and the other four vertices are those of an elongated tetrahedron. Since the polyhedron has twelve (triangular) faces it is also a dodecahedron, hence the alternative names—bisdisphenoidal and dodecahedral—for this type of coordination in crystals.

This is the third dodecahedron we have encountered; details of all three are given in Table 3.

TABLE 3

Faces			Vertices		
f_3	f_4	f_5	v_3	v_4	v_5
12				4	4
	12		8	6	
		12	20		

f_n is the number of n-gon faces, v_p the number of p-connected vertices.

9-coordination

*P.10. *Mono-capped antiprism and tri-capped trigonal prism*

Construct a square antiprism with 5-connectors leaving the spare connectors pointing towards the centres of the square faces. Add a pyramidal cap on one square face to form the *mono-capped square antiprism* (Fig. 16(a)).

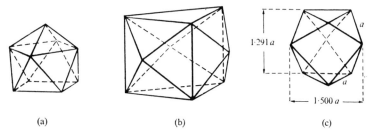

(a)   (b)   (c)

FIG. 16. Mono- and tri-capped trigonal prism.

Add the diagonal of the remaining square face. The polyhedron is now the *tri-capped trigonal prism* (Fig. 16(b)). This 9-coordination group represents the arrangement of H_2O molecules around Nd^{3+} in $[Nd(H_2O)_9](BrO_3)_3$ and of the H atoms around the metal atom in the anion of $K_2(ReH_9)$. This polyhedron is also found as the coordination group in numerous other crystals which provide a striking illustration of the way in which a particular coordination group AX_n can share vertices, edges, or faces to produce structures with a wide range of X : A ratios (Table 4).

TABLE 4. *Examples of the 'tri-capped trigonal prism' coordination group in crystals*

AX_9 sharing	X : A	Examples
—	9	$[Nd(H_2O)_9](BrO_3)_3$, K_2ReH_9
2 edges	7	K_2PaF_7
2 faces	6	$[Sr(H_2O)_6]Cl_2$
2 edges, 4 vertices	5	$LiUF_5$
2 faces, 4 vertices	4	NH_4BiF_4, $NaNdF_4$, $CaTi_2O_4$
2 faces, 6 edges	3	UCl_3
2 faces, 12 edges	2	$PbCl_2$

If a number of these polyhedra are available the models described on p. 114 may be constructed. The polyhedron having all nine vertices equidistant from its centre and all the eighteen edges of Fig. 16(c) equal in length has the dimensions shown in that figure, but for most models the more easily constructed figure built from three half-octahedra will suffice.

12-coordination

P.11. Construct a cuboctahedron with rods and 6-connectors, leaving the spare connectors pointing into the square faces. Insert the face-diagonals shown by heavy lines in Fig. 17 to form an *icosahedron*. This relation between the cuboctahedron and icosahedron is of interest in connection with the closest packing of equal spheres (q.v.).

FIG. 17. Relation between cuboctahedron and icosahedron.

What changes have taken place in the symmetry of the polyhedron?

Another polyhedron with twelve vertices, the truncated tetrahedron, is mentioned on p. 140—see also Table 17 (p. 159).

CYCLIC MOLECULES AND IONS

Cyclic molecules and ions containing various numbers of atoms in the ring are encountered in both inorganic and organic chemistry. We deal here with the types of ring of which most examples are known, namely, 6- and 8-membered rings.

P.12. The 6-ring is planar in C_6H_6, $B_3N_3H_6$, and $B_3N_3H_3Cl_3$, in molecules such as pyridine (C_5H_5N), pyrazine ($C_4H_4N_2$), s-triazine ($C_3H_3N_3$), and simple cyanuric derivatives. In substituted benzenes the ring is probably always approximately planar, but there is appreciable bending of the ring in, for example, di-p-xylylene. In all these molecules the interbond angles in the rings are not far removed from 120°, but the $[(CH_3)_2SiO]_3$ molecule is planar with tetrahedral Si bond angles and O bond angles of 136°.

If the interbond angles have the tetrahedral value, as in cyclohexane (C_6H_{12}), the ring is non-planar, and there are two characteristic forms of the ring, the so-called *chair* and *boat* forms.

Construct a 6-ring with interbond angles of $109\frac{1}{2}°$, and number the atoms consecutively around the ring. Put the ring into the boat configuration with the bonds 2—3 and 5—6 coplanar and atoms 1 and 4 on the bench; atoms 2, 3, 5, and 6 all lie in one plane. If the atoms 3 and 6 are depressed (but not 2 and 5) we obtain a second boat configuration: the bonds 3—4 and 1—6 are coplanar and atoms 1, 6, 3, and 4 are on the bench. Between these two

extremes, which are readily interconvertible, lie the *skew boat* configurations, in which there are no pairs of coplanar bonds. An example is the P_2S_4 ring in $P_2S_6Br_2$, in which two S and two Br atoms occupy at random the four X positions.

Construct a 6-ring in the chair form by making atoms 2, 3, 5, and 6 coplanar and with atoms 1 and 4 on opposite sides of the plane containing the other four atoms. Use tetrahedral bonds and add the extra-annular bonds. Note the disposition of the latter, equatorial and polar, and for a note on the geometrical isomers of substituted ring molecules of this kind see p. 41.

Add three atoms of a different colour representing the O atoms of s-$C_6H_3(OH)_3$, attached to alternate carbon atoms, in the polar positions. The arrangement of these three O atoms is sufficiently similar to that in the PO_4^{3-} ion to permit the formation of the phosphoric ester, which has essentially the same structure as a P_4O_{10} molecule in which the basal P_3O_6 portion has been replaced by a cyclohexane ring.

Note the rigidity of the chair form of the 6-ring, which is the configuration adopted in the solid state by the following molecules and ions: $[BH_2N(CH_3)_2]_3$, $[BH_2P(CH_3)_2]_3$, $(NSCl)_3$, $P_6(C_6H_5)_6$, S_6, $(NH.PO_2)_3^{3-}$, $N_3(SOCl)_2PCl_2$.

*P.13. The stereochemistry of the 8-ring is much more complex. A considerable range of interbond angles is found, from those close to the tetrahedral value (e.g. 108° in S_8) to 123° and 132° for N in $(NSF)_4$ and $[(CH_3)_2SiNH]_4$

respectively and $142°$ in $[(CH_3)_2SiO]_4$. For simplicity we shall assume that all bonds are of the same length (C_8H_8 is an exception) and for the first four models we shall neglect differences in interbond angles, which may be appreciably different for the two atoms in rings A_4B_4.

Planar 8-rings are rare; $(PNF_2)_4$ is an example. Four well-defined configurations of puckered 8-rings may be recognized, in addition to other special or intermediate forms of which we note examples later.

Construct models with tetrahedral bond angles from the following descriptions which indicate the sets of coplanar atoms. The atoms are numbered consecutively around the ring, which should be made from four red and four grey balls, the colours alternating.

Chair: 1, 2, 4, 7 coplanar, 3, 5, 6, 8 coplanar, in parallel planes. This centrosymmetrical form is evidently the analogue of the chair form of the 6-ring. The highest axial symmetry is 2, and maximum symmetry $2/m$.

Boat: 1, 2, 5, 6 coplanar, 3, 4, 7, 8 coplanar, in parallel planes. Highest axial symmetry $\bar{4}$.

Cradle: 1, 3, 5, 7 coplanar, 2, 4, 6, 8 *bisphenoidal*. If the pairs of planes 1, 2, 3– 5, 6, 7 and 3, 4, 5—7, 8, 1 are made parallel, the model represents the molecule of N_4S_4 with short S—S separations 2 –6 and 4—8. Axial symmetry $\bar{4}$. If the model is held in both hands it may readily be twisted into the boat form.

Crown: 1, 3, 5, 7 coplanar, 2, 4, 6, 8 coplanar, the two planes being parallel. Axial symmetry $\bar{8}$ (in crystalline $S_4N_4H_4$, 4 mm).

Examples of molecules and ions with these configurations include:

Chair	Boat	Cradle	Crown
$[(CH_3)_2GaOH]_4$	$(NSF)_4$	N_4S_4	S_8
$[(CH_3)_2SiNH]_4$	$(PNCl_2)_4$	$[(CH_3)_2PN]_4$	$S_4N_4H_4$
	$(NH)_4P_4O_8^{4-}$	$[(CH_3)_2SiNH]_4$	

Note the occurrence of both chair and cradle forms in the same crystal in the case of $[(CH_3)_2SiNH]_4$.

Closely related to the crown configuration is a puckered configuration found for the $[(CH_3)_2SiO]_4$ ring.

Construct the Si_4O_4 ring making Si bond angles tetrahedral and O bond angles $135°$. As for the crown configuration make 1, 3, 5, 7 coplanar and 2, 4, 6, 8 coplanar but with the two planes inclined at an angle of approximately $30°$. Two atoms (say, 1 and 5) now lie on opposite sides of the plane 2, 4, 6, 8. Contrast the planar $[(CH_3)_2SiO]_3$ ring; a planar Si_4O_4 ring having tetrahedral Si bond angles would require O bond angles of $161°$.

The cyclooctatetraene (C_8H_8) molecule adopts a number of different configurations, for example, *boat* in crystalline C_8H_8 and also in $AgNO_3.C_8H_8$, *chair* in $(CO)_3Fe.C_8H_8.Fe(CO)_3$, and a third 'dihedral' form in $(CO)_3Fe.C_8H_8$. The latter has 1, 2, 3, 4, 5, 8 and 5, 6, 7, 8 coplanar.

MOLECULAR SYMMETRY

P.14. The symmetry of a finite object may be described in terms of (*n*-fold) axes of rotation (written 1, 2, 3, etc.) and axes of rotatory inversion ($\bar{1}$, $\bar{2}$, $\bar{3}$, etc.). An object is said to possess an axis of *n*-fold symmetry if its appearance is unchanged after rotation through $360°/n$. An axis of rotatory inversion implies rotation through $360°/n$ accompanied by inversion through the origin *as part of the same operation*. Symmetry operations may be illustrated by diagrams of the type shown in Fig. 18, where black and white commas

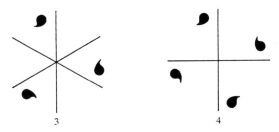

FIG. 18. Operation of 3- and 4-fold axes of symmetry.

represent points above and below the plane of the paper. (An asymmetric object such as a comma is used to avoid introducing other symmetry, such as planes of symmetry, into the diagram.)

By means of diagrams of this kind show that $\bar{1}$ is equivalent to a centre of symmetry, $\bar{2}$ to a plane of symmetry (also represented by the symbol *m*), and $\bar{6}$ to a 3-fold axis plus a plane of symmetry perpendicular to the axis (i.e. in the plane of the paper), written $3/m$.

There is no limitation on the possible types of axial symmetry of finite or of infinite 1-dimensional systems, but the axial symmetry of a pattern that repeats regularly in 2 or 3 dimensions is restricted to 1-, 2-, 3-, 4-, or 6-fold (Appendix 4).

P.15. *Enantiomorphism*

An object is described as enantiomorphic if it cannot be brought into coincidence with its mirror image, that is, it exists in left- and right-handed forms. Molecules or complex ions of this kind have the property of rotating the plane of polarization of plane-polarized light; they are optically active. The criterion for enantiomorphism is the absence of an axis of rotatory inversion. An axis $\bar{n}$ implies a centre of symmetry if n is odd and a plane (or planes) of symmetry if $n = 4p + 2$, and if $n = 4p$ the system can be brought into coincidence with its mirror image. Note that it is the symmetry of the molecule or ion as a whole that is relevant, not the presence or absence of local asymmetry such as 'asymmetric' carbon atoms. Since axes of rotatory inversion $\overline{4p}$ are rare in molecules the condition for enantiomorphism of a molecule is often stated to be the absence of a centre or plane of symmetry.

Construct the carbon–nitrogen skeleton of the tetramethyl-*spiro*-bipyrrollidinium cation (a) with thirteen drilled balls, making all interbond angles equal

(a)   (b)

to $109\frac{1}{2}°$. Determine the number of isomers, and make a sketch of each viewed along the long axis of the molecule showing the directions of the bonds to the methyl groups as at (b). State which of the isomers are enantiomorphic.

P.16. *Dihedral angle*

Any three atoms are coplanar. To define the position of a fourth atom which is not coplanar with the other three we may specify the angle between the planes 123/234 (dihedral angle).

It is important to appreciate the difference between the stereochemistries of molecules such as

and

The molecule aN=Na is planar and exhibits *cis-trans* isomerism, but molecules such as S_2Cl_2 and H_2O_2 are enantiomorphic.

Construct two models of the S_2Cl_2 molecule which differ in having Cl_1 on opposite sides of the plane containing the S atoms and Cl_2. Make the sulphur bond angles and the dihedral angle equal to 90°. Confirm that the two models are related as object and mirror image. The importance of specifying dihedral

angles is well illustrated by the structures of the polysulphide and poly-thionate ions and related molecules.

2. Repeating Patterns: Two-dimensional and Three-dimensional

BEFORE constructing the models described in this chapter it may be found desirable to read Appendices 2 and 3, which form an introduction to 2- and 3-dimensional patterns.

REPEAT UNITS AND FORMULAE

N.1. In order to determine the formula corresponding to an infinite repeating pattern it is necessary to be able to recognize the repeat unit. It should be

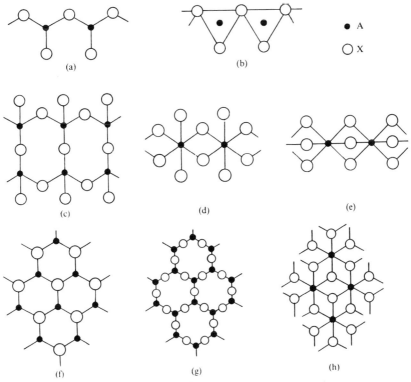

FIG. 19. Examples of 1- and 2-dimensional patterns.

noted that there are alternative ways of representing a structural formula, showing either the atoms and all the bonds or emphasizing the coordination group AX_n around one type of atom and the way in which these groups are linked together by 'sharing' X atoms. For example, the simple chain of Fig. 19(a) may alternatively be drawn as in (b) if it is wished to draw attention to the triangular coordination groups around the A atoms.

Write down the compositions A_mX_n of the chains (c)–(e) and of the layers (f)–(h).

If the coordination groups AX_6 in (d), (e), and (h) are octahedral, how are the octahedra joined together?

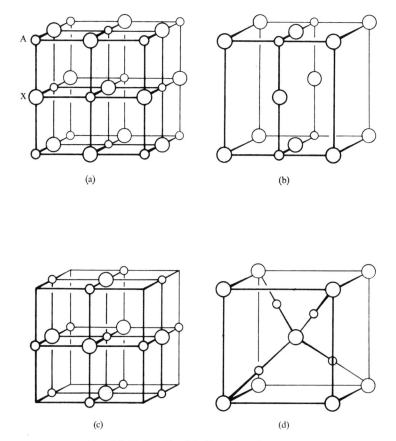

FIG. 20. Unit cells of 3-dimensional structures.

N.2. 3-dimensional patterns

A diagram of the unit cell of a pattern does not necessarily convey much idea of the nature of the pattern, as may be seen from Fig. 123 (p. 166) which shows unit cells of the plane hexagonal net. This is, of course, also true of 3D patterns, but nevertheless it is conventional (and often convenient) to show only one unit cell of a crystal structure. In relating the atoms shown in such a diagram to the true unit cell content (or formula), it is important to remember that only an atom in the interior of the cell belongs completely and exclusively to that cell. Atoms in a face, on an edge, or at a corner, belong to 2, 4, or 8 cells respectively, and therefore count only as $\frac{1}{2}$, $\frac{1}{4}$, or $\frac{1}{8}$ atoms per cell.

What is the content of the unit cells in Fig. 20? Name the structures and describe the arrangements of nearest neighbours around A and X atoms in each structure.

THE GEOMETRY OF THE 3-CONNECTED 6-GON LAYER

N.3. If all the interbond angles are equal this layer is strictly planar only if all the angles are 120°, as in graphite and BN. In other crystals interbond angles in the range 90–$109\frac{1}{2}$° are found, and the configuration of this layer for

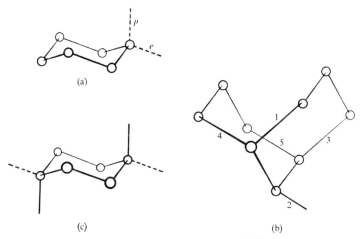

(a)

(c)   (b)

FIG. 21. Geometry of the 3-connected 6-gon layer.

such bond angles is of some interest. For convenience we shall use the tetrahedral value ($109\frac{1}{2}$°). We have seen that when the isolated 6-ring is non-planar it is usually chair-shaped. This configuration is also the one found in non-planar hexagonal layers in crystals.

Construct a 6-ring from drilled balls and spokes in the *chair* configuration, using tetrahedral angles between the bonds. Note the alternative directions for the third bond from each atom, namely, *e* (approximately in the mean plane of the ring) and *p* (perpendicular to the mean plane of the ring)—see Fig. 21(a). The numbers of possible combinations of *e* and *p* bonds for the ring as a whole are evidently the same as the numbers of substituted benzenes. Indicating the number of p positions by the superscript numeral, these numbers are:

$$\left. \begin{array}{l} p^1 \text{ and } p^5, \text{ one each,} \\ p^2 \text{ and } p^4, \text{ three each,} \\ p^3, \qquad\qquad \text{three,} \end{array} \right\} \text{total 11}$$

With the arrangements p^0 (e^6) and p^6 there are thirteen different ways of arranging the six extra-annular bonds.

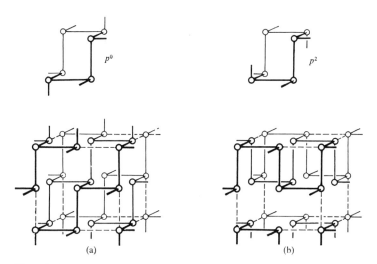

(a)   (b)

FIG. 22. Relation of the structures of As and black P to the simple cubic structure.

It can be shown (by trial) that if we require all rings to be chair-shaped *with the same disposition of bonds from each*, then only three of these combinations lead to periodic layers. (It is possible to eliminate seven bond arrangements simply on the grounds that the sequence $-p-p-p-$ in one ring implies $-p-e-p-$ in an adjacent ring. This may be seen from the model (Fig. 21(b)) in which the bonds 1—2—3 are $p-e-p$ for the left-hand ring and the bonds 4—2—5 are $p-p-p$ for the right-hand ring.)

The three permissible bond arrangements are p^0 (e^6), p^1, and the centro-symmetrical p^2 (Fig. 21(c)).

Build portions of the 6-gon layer for p^0, p^1, and p^2, and sketch elevations of the layers. It may be found preferable to make the p^0 layer first and then the p^2 layer. Make two p^2 rings and check that there is only one way of combining them so that each remains p^2.

No example is yet known of the p^1 layer. The p^0 layer is that found in crystalline As, Sb, and Bi (and the low-temperature form of GeTe), and p^2

is the layer in black P and the isostructural GeS, SnS, GeSe, and SnSe. The p^2 layer is in fact more buckled than in our model, for the interbond angles in black phosphorus (two of $102°$ and one of $96\frac{1}{2}°$) are appreciably smaller than the angle ($109\frac{1}{2}°$) used in the model.

When the layers are stacked in the crystal each atom has three next-nearest neighbours in the adjacent layer, and both the As and black P structures may be regarded as distorted simple cubic structures (or for the binary compounds, distorted NaCl structures). These structures are illustrated in this way in Fig. 22, which is diagrammatic in that all the interbond angles have been made equal to $90°$.

THREE-DIMENSIONAL NETS

The cubic 3-connected (10, 3) net

N.4. In the most symmetrical configuration of this net (Fig. 128(a)) the three links from each point are equal in length and the interbond angles are $120°$, i.e the three links from any point are coplanar. The net then has cubic symmetry. The 3- and 4-fold axes are all screw axes, and the model is most conveniently constructed from helical chains as sub-units.

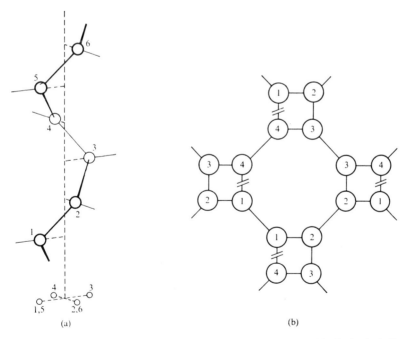

FIG. 23. The 3-dimensional (10, 3) net with cubic symmetry: (a) single 4_1 helix, (b) projection of four helices.

With three bonds at $120°$ from each ball make four identical helical chains of six balls, each corresponding to Fig. 23(a), in which the figures indicate the translations of successive points along the helix. (It is not possible to make a rigid model with sufficient connections between the helices unless at least two of them extend to six points along the 4_1 axis.) Arrange the helices with their axes vertical and join them together, as shown in Fig. 23(b), by the horizontal links 1–1, 2–2, etc., removing duplicate links. Note that the link 4–//–1 joins 4 to the fifth point of the helix, which lies vertically above 1. Two links from each ball are used in the helix; the remaining links from successive balls should be perpendicular to the axis of the helix and related by rotations through $90°$.

Check that all the circuits are 10-gons, and confirm the cubic symmetry by locating the other sets of 4_1 axes and also the 3_1 axes. Draw a projection of the net viewed along a 3_1 axis. In how many directions do the (a) 4_1, (b) 3_1 axes run?

Note that the net is completely specified by the group of four points in one helix ($Z_t = 4$) but that the cubic unit cell for this special configuration of the net contains a larger number of points. What is this number? The cubic symmetry disappears if the net is distorted but properties dependent solely on the topology of the net are not affected since all the connections are maintained. If a sufficiently large portion of the net can be built determine the numbers of 10-gons to which each point and each link is common.

Since all the helices are either left- or right-handed the net as a whole is enantiomorphic.

The diamond net

N.5. This may be constructed in two different ways, each of which illustrates a particular point concerning the net.

(a) Take a number of *pairs* of atoms with tetrahedral bonds arranged in the *staggered* configuration. It is convenient to insert all four spokes in each ball. Join pairs together (removing duplicated spokes as necessary) keeping all pairs *in the same orientation in space.* Building the model in this way illustrates that the topological repeat unit of the diamond net is a pair of points (atoms), or $Z_t = 2$. If a sufficiently large portion of the diamond net is available find the cubic unit cell ($Z_c = 8$) and make a sketch-plan. Note the configuration of the 6-gon rings of which the net is composed.

(b) Alternatively start from a single point and build outwards in all directions simply ensuring a staggered arrangement of bonds from all pairs of adjacent points. Although the structure is built radially it is periodic in three dimensions. It is interesting that this property of the diamond net is paralleled in two dimensions by the 3-connected net built of 6-gons which represents the structure of a sheet of atoms in the other polymorph of carbon, graphite.

*N.6. *Some borate structures based on the diamond net*

Numerous examples of crystal structures based on the diamond net were given in Table 2 (p. 19). This net represents the simplest 3D arrangement of single atoms forming tetrahedral bonds or of tetrahedral groups that can share all their vertices with other similar groups. We study here the relation to the diamond net of the structures of a number of anhydrous crystalline borates which were included in this table.

Construct models of the borate ions (a)–(c) from drilled balls and spokes using tetrahedral or trigonal planar bonds for the two kinds of boron atom and interbond angles of 120° for the oxygen atoms in the rings. Make the rings in (a) and (c) approximately planar.

(a)

(b)

(c)

Note the spatial arrangement of the four OH groups in each ion. These ions exist as discrete hydroxy-borate ions in crystals of certain borates crystallized from aqueous solution. In a number of anhydrous borates the anions consist of 3D frameworks built from cyclic units of the types (a)–(c). These units are joined through oxygen atoms (in the positions of the OH groups in the above formulae) each of which is shared between two similar units to form a diamond-like 3D framework.

What are the compositions of the anions?

What is the composition of the anion formed from equal numbers of (a) and (c) units alternating in a diamond-like framework?

The (3, 4)-connected net of Fig. 128(b) (p. 172)

N.7. This net may be derived by replacing one-half of the points in the diamond net by pairs of 3-connected points. The following method of construction is equivalent to, but more convenient than, making the substitution in an actual model of the diamond net.

Make up a number of units in which the planes defined by the bonds *ab* and *de* (Fig. 24) are perpendicular. Use red balls. Join four of these units to

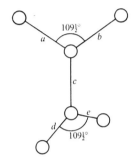

FIG. 24. Unit for (3, 4)-connected net.

a grey ball forming tetrahedral bonds, arranging the units so that all the bonds of type *c* are parallel. The structure may then be continued, grey balls alternating with the double units, all the latter maintaining the same orientation.

Compare the model with the unit cell shown in Fig. 128(b) and the values of Z, n, and y with those in Table 18 (p. 171).

The 3-connected net of Fig. 128(e) (p. 172)

N.8. Now replace the 4-connected points in the previous model by pairs of points (Fig. 24), still maintaining all links of type *c* parallel.

Compare the model with the unit cell shown in Fig. 128(e) (p. 172) and the values of Z and n with those for the cubic (10, 3) net. Study of this net shows that all the links are not equivalent, all those of type *c* having a different environment from those forming the zigzag chains. A more precise description of the difference is given by the values of y for the two types of link.

FURTHER STUDY OF 4-CONNECTED 3D NETS

The most symmetrical arrangement of four bonds in a plane is the square planar configuration and in three dimensions it is the regular tetrahedral configuration. Both bond arrangements, alone and in combination, lead to 3D nets, and certain less symmetrical variants are also of interest. In considering the latter it is convenient to regard them as intermediate between the square planar arrangement and the other limiting case where the four bonds form two collinear pairs of coincident bonds ($=\cdot=$).

Starting with four points in a plane equidistant from the origin we raise and lower alternate points (Fig. 25). This represents the operation of an axis of 4-fold rotatory inversion ($\bar{4}$). The interbond angles are two of $\theta°$ and four of $\phi°$. Initially the values are $\theta = 180°$ and $\phi = 90°$ (all points coplanar). All six angles become equal if $\theta = \phi = 109°28'$, the regular tetrahedral arrangement. The other limiting case would arise when θ becomes zero, A and C

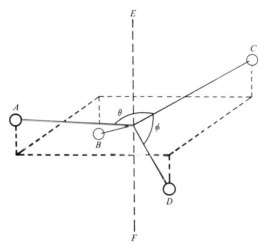

FIG. 25. Operation of $\bar{4}$ axis.

coinciding at E, and B and D at F. If we are interested in arrangements of four *atoms* around a central one small values of θ are not realizable, since atoms have size. However, a number of intermediate cases are important:

θ (two)	180°	140	120	six of	$97\frac{1}{2}$	90	0
ϕ (four)	90°	97	104	$109\frac{1}{2}$	115	120	180
	Square planar bonds (b)	Flattened tetrahedral bonds in certain Cu^{II} compounds		(a)	(d)	(c)	Two collinear bonds

The three simplest 4-connected 3D nets are those in which *all* points have the bond arrangements (a), (b), or (c), namely:

polygons

(a) diamond }
(b) NbO } 6-gons
(c) 'Fedorov' net   4- and 6-gons

We shall also construct a model of

(d) PtS   4- and 8-gons

In this crystal the bond angles of the S atom are two of $97\frac{1}{2}°$ and four of $115°$, but in order to build the model from the standard drilled balls we shall make the angles $90°$ and $120°$ respectively. This is the simplest net in which equal numbers of points form four coplanar and four tetrahedral bonds. As a further example of a net of this general type we shall also describe the structure of PdP_2, in which one-third of the atoms (Pd) form four coplanar and two-thirds (P) form tetrahedral bonds.

Interpenetrating diamond nets

N.9. Construct a portion of the diamond net maintaining a staggered arrangement of the tetrahedral bonds from all pairs of adjacent atoms. Make a second net with balls of a different colour completely interpenetrating the first net, using additional bonds where necessary to hold the two nets together in the same orientation with atoms of one midway between appropriate pairs of atoms of the other net.

Find the unit cell of this composite structure: (a) if the differently coloured balls represent atoms of different elements, and (b) if all atoms are of the same kind. Answer the following questions for case (a) and case (b). Is the structure body-centred? What is the volume of the unit cell compared with the unit cell of a single diamond net? Give examples of crystals with structure (a) or (b).

Sketch the unit cell of the structure consisting of two interpenetrating diamond nets but having X atoms midway along each bond forming two collinear bonds to the A atoms. What is the formula? Give examples of compounds crystallizing with this structure.

N.10. Investigate the result of assembling tetrahedrally bonded atoms if the *eclipsed* configuration is maintained at every pair of adjacent atoms.

Wurtzite structure

N.11. Join two atoms with their tetrahedral bonds in the *eclipsed* position. Add further atoms making the bond arrangement *staggered* about all bonds except those parallel to the first bond. Build sufficient of the structure to identify the unit cell, sketch the cell, and determine the number of atoms in it and their coordinates. What is the name of this structure? Give examples of compounds which adopt the structure.

The Fedorov net

N.12. Check that for the bond arrangement of Fig. 26(a) the most symmetrical relations between the bonds from two adjacent points are those shown at (b)–(e). To obtain this bond arrangement use holes of type E in Fig. 10 (p. 21) in the drilled balls. We investigate (b) and (d). In Fig. 26 (b)–(e) the bonds shown as heavy lines are coplanar.

Construct a model maintaining the fully eclipsed arrangement (b) for each pair of adjacent atoms, and use red and grey balls alternately. Instead of producing 5-gon rings as when the interbond angles are close to 108° the atoms now form plane 4-gons and 6-gons, and the net corresponds to the vertices and edges of the polyhedra in Fedorov's space-filling by truncated

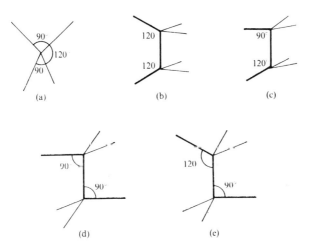

FIG. 26. Bond arrangements in 4-connected nets (see text).

octahedra. The points of this net are the positions of Si or Al atoms in the aluminosilicates of the sodalite or ultramarine type, the polyhedral cavities accommodating the cations or other anions which do not form part of the $(Si,Al)O_2$ framework.

In forming an AX_2 framework in this way we have added an X atom between each pair of adjacent A atoms, that is, we have placed SiO_4 or AlO_4 tetrahedra at the points of the net and joined them by sharing all vertices (O atoms). In the actual crystals the oxygen atoms lie off the links of the net in order to give oxygen bond angles in the range 130–150° rather than 180°. ***N.13.** Now consider the net as an assembly of tetrahedra, each consisting of four grey balls (X atoms) surrounding a red ball (A atom). Since there are equal numbers of grey and red balls the composition is clearly AX. Each AX_4 tetrahedron shares a pair of opposite edges with neighbouring ones, and these chains of tetrahedra, in three mutually perpendicular directions, are joined by vertex-sharing to form the 3D framework. This framework has not been found as a crystal structure, probably because there is considerable distortion of the tetrahedra from regularity. The impossibility of building this structure with regular tetrahedra can be demonstrated in the following way.

Using 3-connectors, make six pairs of edge-sharing tetrahedra and then join vertices *C* of each pair to vertices *B* of other pairs (Fig. 27) so that each vertex is common to three tetrahedra. The vertices *D* are unshared, and the twelve tetrahedra form an icosahedral group. Comparison of this model with the Fedorov net will show that regular icosahedral units of this kind will not join up to form a repeating 3D structure.

Calculate the relative lengths of the shared and unshared edges of the tetrahedron which will form the 3D framework corresponding to the Fedorov net. (Note that one-half of the vertices of a truncated octahedron are the

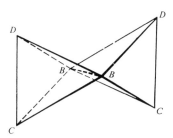

FIG. 27. Edge-sharing tetrahedra for icosahedral group.

vertices of an icosahedron; these (non-regular) icosahedra and (non-regular) tetrahedra together fill space.) What is the ratio of the numbers of tetrahedra to icosahedra?

If an atom (or group) M occupies each of the truncated octahedral cavities and X atoms all the points of the Fedorov net, what is the formula?

The 'pseudo-diamond' net

*N.14. Assemble balls and spokes maintaining the staggered relation (d) of Fig. 26 between the bonds from each pair of adjacent balls. (There is a centre of symmetry at the mid-point of every link.) The structure formed is similar to the diamond net, but in each chair-shaped ring one pair of opposite angles are right-angles while the remaining ones are angles of 120°.

This structure has only tetragonal symmetry. What is the axial ratio c : a of the cell containing eight points corresponding to the cubic unit cell of the normal diamond structure?

The NbO net

N.15. We have seen that for atoms forming four tetrahedral bonds ($109\frac{1}{2}°$) the requirement of the 'staggered' relation between bonds from adjacent atoms leads, without any further conditions, to the diamond structure. If there are four coplanar bonds from each atom and the bonds from adjacent atoms lie in perpendicular planes the resulting net is, like the diamond net, built of 6-gon rings with the chair configuration but with interbond angles of 90°.

Construct a portion of this net as indicated above with alternate atoms of different colours. The sole example of this structure is NbO.

(i) To which AX structure is it related, and what is the relationship?

(ii) Which are the *next* nearest neighbours of a Nb atom, and how does the Nb–Nb distance compare with Nb–O?

The PtS structure

N.16. This model is built of two types of atom with different bond arrangements, namely, Pt atoms forming four coplanar bonds and S atoms forming four tetrahedral bonds. For S use the tetrahedral arrangement with two opposite bond angles of 90° (and four of 120°), and use balls of two different colours for Pt and S. Build a short portion of planar chain using one of the

90° angles of S in the chain. The model may then be extended by forming similar chains at right-angles to the first. Make enough of the model to check that it repeats in three dimensions.

The most symmetrical form of this structure, with tetragonal symmetry, is adopted by PtS and PtO, and less symmetrical forms by PdS and CuO. For convenience we have used interbond angles of 90° (2) and 120° (4) for S. This is not the preferred bond arrangement for S or O, but it will be clear from the model that it is not possible to have 90° bond angles for the metal and at the same time *regular* tetrahedral bonds from S (O). The angle α is not only the supplement of the Pt bond angle in a planar chain of this kind but is also one of the tetrahedral bond angles of S. The value found in crystals with this structure represents a compromise between the bonding requirements of the two kinds of atoms.

The PdP₂ net

*N.17. In crystalline PdP₂ all atoms form four bonds, those from Pd being coplanar and those from P tetrahedral. The 3D net representing this structure may conveniently be constructed from the (3,4)-connected 5-gon layer of Fig. 28(b), the 3-connected points in adjacent layers being subsequently joined together to make all points 4-connected.

Start with a pair of red balls forming tetrahedral bonds and join them in the staggered configuration. Attach two grey balls (each forming four square coplanar bonds) to each and arrange the four grey balls at the corners of a plane rectangle. The red balls lie above and below the line joining mid-points of opposite sides of the rectangle and have their fourth bonds lying to opposite sides of the plane of the rectangle (Fig. 28(a)). Four pentagons may now be completed by adding red balls (shaded circles) as in Fig. 28(b), which shows

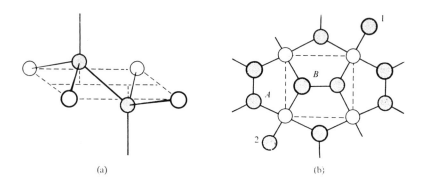

(a)   (b)

FIG. 28. Construction of model of PdP$_2$ structure.

a normal projection of the (puckered) layer. Red balls shown as heavy or light circles have their fourth (free) bond pointing above or below the plane of the projection respectively.

Make a second layer identical to the first. Since the pattern of free bonds from red balls is the same on both sides of a layer, two layers fit together if related by the translation AB. A more rigid model is made if a further red ball (1) is added to the lower layer and (2) to the upper layer.

Check that one-third of the atoms (Pd) in the structure form coplanar and the remainder (P) tetrahedral bonds. Note the continuous chains of P atoms.

REPRESENTATION OF STRUCTURES BY PROJECTIONS

N.18. It is useful to be able to visualize or construct models of structures from plans and elevations.

From the plans shown in Fig. 29 deduce (i) the number of equidistant nearest neighbours of an atom and (ii) the number of atoms in the unit cell, which in each case is a cube.

Describe or name the structures and indicate on sketches the bonds from one atom to its nearest neighbours.

With drilled balls and spokes construct models of (c)–(f).

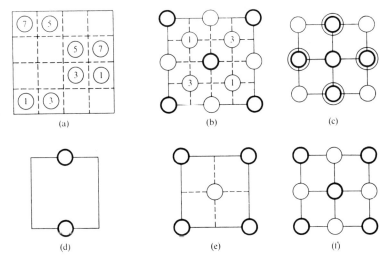

FIG. 29. Projections of unit cells. Heavy circles represent atoms at height 0 (i.e. in the plane of the projection) and light circles atoms at height $c/2$ where c is the length of the edge of the cubic cell. The numbers indicate heights above the plane of the projection in terms of $c/8$ in (a) and $c/4$ in (b).

3. Sphere Packings

THE CLOSEST PACKING OF EQUAL SPHERES

THREE spheres are most closely packed if each touches the other two. Their centres are at the corners of an equilateral triangle, and evidently equal spheres are most closely packed in a plane if their centres lie at the points of the 6-connected triangular net. The closest packing of equal spheres in three dimensions presents a more interesting problem. The densest arrangement of four spheres, at the vertices of a regular tetrahedron, cannot be repeated to

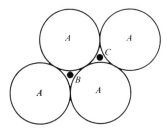

FIG. 30. The closest packing of equal spheres (see text).

fill space because the dihedral angle of a tetrahedron (70°32′) is not an exact submultiple of 360°. The greatest number of equal spheres that can be arranged around and in contact with a similar sphere is twelve, and the most symmetrical arrangement of the twelve spheres is an icosahedral one. Since the edge of a regular icosahedron is 5 per cent greater than the distance from vertex to centre the spheres of an icosahedral shell are not in contact with one another. It is not possible to pack equal spheres to form a regular periodic structure in which each sphere has twelve nearest neighbours arranged at the vertices of a regular icosahedron, though it is possible to continue adding layers of spheres to an icosahedral shell around a central sphere. This icosahedral sphere packing is not periodic in three dimensions but is a structure radiating from a unique centre, and moreover its density (fraction of space occupied by the spheres) is only 0·6882. Such a packing can, by slight movements of the spheres, rearrange to one of greater density. The same density (0·7405) can be attained by stacking close-packed (c.p.) layers of the kind described above. Spheres of one layer fit into the hollows of adjacent layers, that is, if the spheres of one layer are those labelled A in Fig. 30 those of adjacent layers have their centres above B or C. In such sphere stackings

each sphere has twelve equidistant neighbours. Because of the alternative positions available for each layer there is an indefinite number of c.p. layer
sequences. A convenient nomenclature describes a layer as h or c type
according to whether the layers on each side of it are of the same or different
kinds, i.e.

$$A \ B \ A \qquad A \ B \ C \qquad A \ B \ A \ C \ A \ B \ A \ C \dots$$
$$h \qquad\qquad c \qquad\qquad h \ c \ h \ c \ h \ c$$

The symbols h and c for the two simplest types of closest packing, namely,

$$A \ B \ A \ B \ A \ B \dots \qquad\qquad A \ B \ C \ A \ B \ C \dots$$
$$h \qquad\qquad\qquad\qquad c$$

hexagonal close-packing   cubic close-packing
(h.c.p.)   (c.c.p.)

derive from the crystallographic symmetries of the resulting assemblies of
spheres.

S.1. Determine the unit cell of h.c.p. from a model consisting of parts of
three layers, the spheres of the third layer being placed directly above those
of the first. Draw a plan of the unit cell, give the coordinates of the atoms and
the number of atoms in the cell.

Identify a unit cell in a c.c.p. assembly consisting of portions of four layers,
the fourth layer being a repeat of the first. How many atoms does it contain?

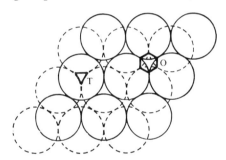

FIG. 31. Tetrahedral and octahedral holes between close-packed spheres.

Closest packing of equal spheres of one kind represents the crystal structures of the rare gases and the majority of metals. In many crystals, notably
those of metallic halides and oxides, the anions are appreciably larger than
the metal ions, the latter occupying the relatively small interstices among the
c.p. anions. Apart from the very small holes surrounded by a triangle of c.p.
atoms these interstices are of two kinds. The smallest holes surrounded by a
polyhedral group of c.p. atoms are those marked T in Fig. 31. An atom in a
hole of this kind has four c.p. neighbours whose centres lie at the vertices of
a regular tetrahedron. The larger holes (O) are surrounded by octahedral
groups of six c.p. atoms.

Determine from models the ratios of the numbers of T and O holes to the number of spheres in an infinite assembly of c.p. spheres.

If the radius of a c.p. sphere is unity, what are the radii of atoms which exactly fit into the tetrahedral and octahedral interstices?

We describe first a few small finite groups of c.p. spheres and then proceed to structures in which the close-packing extends indefinitely in three dimensions. We shall not consider systematically those structures in which various fractions of the total number of tetrahedral interstices are occupied. It is possible to describe a number of simple structures in this way (see, for example, Table 5, p. 58). However, in many crystals of this type the bonds have appreciable covalent character, that is, the metal atom is forming four directed (tetrahedral) bonds. We have therefore described the structures of the two forms of ZnS under 3D 4-connected nets, and we shall include other structures (PbO, red HgI_2) under 'Structures built from tetrahedra' (p. 76).

Structures in which metal atoms occupy octahedral holes will be considered in two groups. In addition to compounds A_mX_n in which all the c.p. atoms are X atoms there are crystals in which atoms of two (or more) kinds form the c.p. assembly. Such atoms must be of similar size, for example, Ba^{2+} and O^{2-} (in complex oxides), Cs^+ and Cl^- (in complex halides), or Cl^- and OH^- (in hydroxyhalides). Small metal atoms (ions) occupy some or all of the octahedral interstices among the anions. We shall describe a number of structures of this kind.

SOME FINITE GROUPS OF CLOSE-PACKED ATOMS

The most compact grouping of four equal spheres is the tetrahedral one. It can be identified in periodic closest packings, which can be built up from such groups, as shown in Fig. 32(a). Tetrahedral molecules AX_4 can

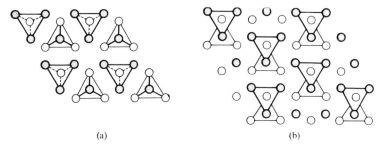

(a)   (b)

FIG. 32. Closest packing of X atoms in crystals consisting of molecules (a) AX_4 and (b) A_2X_6.

accordingly be packed together in a crystal so that the X atoms are close-packed. This is also true of groups of six atoms forming two tetrahedra sharing an edge, as in the Al_2Br_6 molecule in crystalline aluminium bromide (Fig. 32(b)).

S.2. Draw sketches of the same type as Fig. 32(a) and (b) showing how the following groups can pack to form a periodic close-packed assembly: (a) octahedral X_6 groups and (b) X_{10} groups consisting of two octahedra sharing an edge. These represent possible ways of packing molecules AX_6 or A_2X_{10} in crystals.

What are the fractions of the total numbers of tetrahedral or octahedral holes occupied by A atoms in 3D packings of (i) AX_4, (ii) A_2X_6, (iii) AX_6, and (iv) A_2X_{10} molecules of the types described above?

S.3. The following groupings can be constructed from the units listed on p. 22, to which we refer as 3S, 6S, and 7S units. In all the models of this section adjacent units are to be placed together in such a way as to make the maximum number of contacts between spheres.

(a) Place a 3S unit on a 6S unit. If the three tetrahedral holes are occupied by A atoms, how are the AX_4 tetrahedra joined together? Give examples of A_3X_9 molecules or ions with this structure and write down the usual structural formula.

(b) Add a tenth sphere to complete a tetrahedral group of ten X atoms. If all the tetrahedral holes are occupied by A atoms, what is the formula and what molecule does the structure represent? What is the type of close-packing? (For c.p. groups of nineteen and twenty-eight atoms, see p. 87.)

(c) Place together two 6S units related by a rotation of 60° and add a single sphere beyond the centre of each unit. The model can be held together by holding one of these single spheres in each hand. Describe and sketch the model, showing the centres of the spheres.

(d) Put together 3S, 7S, and 3S units (in that order) with the second 3S unit rotated through 60° relative to the first. This model shows the complete group of twelve neighbours around the central atom in cubic close-packing. It also represents a unit cell of c.c.p. Sketch the unit cell. How is it related to the unit cell made in (c)? What is the name of the coordination polyhedron?

Note that this is not the most symmetrical arrangement of twelve neighbours, the faces of the polyhedron being squares and equilateral triangles. An icosahedral arrangement has higher symmetry but does not lead to a periodic 3D sphere packing.

(e) Put together 7S, 6S, and 3S units in this order. This group of sixteen spheres shows all four planes of closest packed atoms in cubic close-packing. Name the polyhedron whose vertices are the centres of the outermost twelve spheres of the group.

(f) In order to study the addition of further spheres to the group of sixteen made in (e) it is convenient to hold the three units together with an elastic band. A further 6S unit may be added on each hexagonal face of the truncated tetrahedral group in one of two ways. The first continues the cubic close-packing of the sixteen spheres, and forms a group of forty c.c.p. spheres. The second possibility is to place each outer layer in the h.c.p. relation to the previous layers. This group of forty spheres is not part of a periodic close-packing. It represents the arrangement of oxygen atoms in the $PW_{12}O_{40}$ and related heteropolyacid ions. (For h.c.p. and all other more complex types of close-packing the sequence of c.p. layers is maintained in one direction only—perpendicular to the c.p. layers. The only periodic 3D sphere packing having c.p. layers in four inclined directions is cubic close-packing.)

STRUCTURES A_mX_n IN WHICH X ATOMS ARE CLOSE-PACKED AND A ATOMS OCCUPY TETRAHEDRAL INTERSTICES

For reasons stated earlier we shall not derive systematically the structures in which various fractions of the total number of tetrahedral interstices are occupied in c.p. assemblies. The simpler structures which are related in this purely geometrical way are listed in Table 5. There are, however, certain general points relating to these structures which may be noted here.

TABLE 5. *Structures with tetrahedral coordination of A and close-packing of X atoms*

Fraction of tetrahedral holes occupied	Sequence of c.p. layers		Formula	C.N.s of A and X
	AB ...	ABC ...		
All	—	Li_2O (antifluorite)	A_2X	4 : 8
3/4	—	O_3Mn_2	A_3X_2	4 : 6
1/2	ZnS (wurtzite)	ZnS (zinc-blende) PtS PbO	AX	4 : 4
1/4	β-ZnCl$_2$	HgI$_2$ and γ-ZnCl$_2$ SiS$_2$ OCu$_2$ α-ZnCl$_2$	AX$_2$	4 : 2
1/6	Al$_2$Br$_6$	—	AX$_3$	
1/8	SnBr$_4$	SnI$_4$	AX$_4$	4 : 1

S.4. The antifluorite structure of Li_2O may be described as a c.p. assembly of O^{2-} ions in which Li^+ ions occupy all the tetrahedral interstices (see also p. 75).

Observe the relative positions of tetrahedral holes in a h.c.p. assembly and show why no compounds adopt the h.c.p. structure in which *all* tetrahedral holes are occupied.

There are no layer structures in Table 5 in which the A_mX_n layers are parallel to the planes of c.p. X atoms. In the (unknown) AX layer structure in which all tetrahedral holes are occupied between alternate pairs of c.p. layers each AX_4 tetrahedron shares three edges, and every X is bonded to four A atoms. The model is more conveniently built from tetrahedra and is therefore described on p. 84.

Describe the relation between the tetrahedral AX_4 groups if A atoms occupy *in the most regular way* one-half of the tetrahedral holes between a pair of c.p. layers. (A model may also be made from tetrahedra for comparison.) Suggest a reason why this structure, which may be described as the tetrahedral analogue of the CdI_2 layer, is not adopted by any compound AX_2, and compare this layer with those of HgI_2 (red) and AlOCl (pp. 139 and 141, respectively).

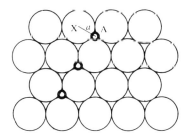

FIG. 33. Construction of model of HgI_2 (red) structure.

S.5. Place a row of small spheres (A atoms) on a c.p. layer in the positions of the small circles in Fig. 33 and make two other similar layers. Stack these composite layers so that each is displaced relative to the one below by the translation a, that is, the atoms A associated with one layer lie above the X atoms of the layer below.

Observe that the A atoms lie at the points of a square net, the plane of which is inclined to that of the c.p. layers, and that the AX_4 tetrahedra share vertices. This is the layer of the red form of HgI_2.

STRUCTURES A_mX_n IN WHICH X ATOMS ARE CLOSE-PACKED AND A ATOMS OCCUPY OCTAHEDRAL INTERSTICES

S.6. Consider one c.p. layer. The positions indicated by the small circles in Fig. 34 become octahedral holes if the atoms of the next c.p. layer fall over the positions marked by the crosses. Place a coloured ball in position A and observe that if any of the six nearest octahedral sites are occupied (small open circles) this implies sharing of edges of octahedral groups. If only the sites shown as filled circles (one-third of the total) are occupied between any pair

of adjacent c.p. layers there are no edges or vertices shared between octahedra
at this level. Whether vertices, edges, or faces are shared in the final structure
will depend on the relation between the sets of octahedral sites occupied
between successive pairs of layers. We shall see that this in turn determines
the sequence of c.p. layers, or, alternatively, the sequence of c.p. layers determines the relation between the AX_6 octahedra.

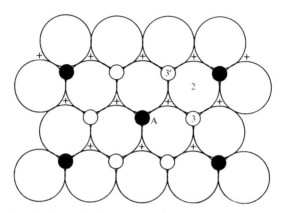

FIG. 34. Octahedral holes between close-packed spheres.

Occupation of more than one-third of the octahedral sites between a pair
of c.p. layers implies edge-sharing. The most symmetrical ways of filling one-
half or two-thirds of these sites are shown in Figs. 35 and 36. Since the number
of octahedral sites in a c.p. assembly is equal to the number of c.p. spheres the
formulae corresponding to occupation of one-third, one-half, and two-thirds
of the octahedral sites between *every* pair of adjacent layers are AX_3, AX_2, and
A_2X_3. If these fractions of the total number of octahedral holes are occupied
between *alternate* pairs of c.p. layers the formulae are AX_6, AX_4, and AX_3.
The last of these three possibilities corresponds to the $CrCl_3$ or BiI_3 layer.
The formula corresponding to occupation of all the octahedral holes in a c.p.
assembly is AX, the structures being those of NaCl and NiAs for cubic and
hexagonal close-packing respectively. If all the octahedral holes are filled
between alternate pairs of c.p. layers the analogous structures are those of
$CdCl_2$ and CdI_2 ($Mg(OH)_2$).

What is the nature of the A–X complex when the sites occupied between
alternate pairs of c.p. layers are the small black circles of Figs. 34 and 35(a)?

Construct portions of the $CrCl_3$ and $CdCl_2$ layers and describe the relations
between the AX_6 coordination groups.

We now study the structures in which the following proportions of octahedral sites are occupied between *all* successive pairs of c.p. layers: one-third,
one-half, two-thirds, and all the sites.

One-third of the octahedral sites occupied

S.7. Place A atoms (coloured balls) on the upper surface of a c.p. layer in the positions of the small filled circles of Fig. 34. Place a second c.p. layer over the first so that the centres of the spheres of the second layer fall above the points marked by the crosses in Fig. 34.

(i) We could place the A atoms in contact with the upper surface of the second c.p. layer vertically above those already in position. Repetition of this arrangement gives columns of octahedral AX_6 groups sharing opposite faces, i.e. infinite chain molecules of composition AX_3 (ZrI_3 structure). Note that the positions chosen for the A atoms determine the sequence of c.p. layers, that is, a column of octahedra sharing opposite faces implies *hexagonal* close-packing.

(ii) Starting with two c.p. layers and the five A atoms between them as in Fig. 34 try the next set of positions for A atoms above the second c.p. layer, the positions marked (?), which are vertically above the first layer of c.p. atoms. If the same relative translation is maintained between successive layers of A atoms, what is the type of close-packing and the nature of the structure as regards the sharing of octahedral vertices, edges, or faces? Make a sketch showing how the octahedra are linked together.

(iii) From the topological standpoint one of the simplest structures for a compound AX_3 is one in which each octahedral AX_6 group shares its vertices with six other similar groups. The underlying framework is the simplest 6-connected 3D net, the primitive (P) lattice of the crystallographer. The most symmetrical configuration of this structure has full cubic symmetry, the A atoms lying at the points of the simple cubic lattice and the X atoms midway along the edges of the cubic unit cell. It is noteworthy that this highly symmetrical structure is adopted by only one trioxide (ReO_3—the forms of WO_3 have less symmetrical structures while MoO_3 has an entirely different structure described on p. 107) and by a minority of the numerous transition metal trifluorides (those of Nb, Ta, and Mo).

We show below that a structure of this topological type is possible for h.c.p. X atoms but not possible for c.c.p. X atoms. In ReO_3 the O atoms occupy three-quarters of the positions of c.c.p. Owing to the existence of this less densely packed structure there is the possibility of structures intermediate between the ReO_3 structure and the h.c.p. structure of RhF_3, and such structures are in fact adopted by FeF_3, CoF_3, etc.

We have seen that the pattern of A atom sites indicated by the small filled circles of Fig. 34 is the *only* way of filling one-third of the octahedral holes if only vertex-sharing is permitted. This pattern of sites must be occupied between every pair of adjacent c.p. layers. As before, place the second c.p. layer over the first with the A atoms in place between the layers. The only permissible positions for A atoms above the second layer are those of type (3), or the symmetrically equivalent (3′), if only vertex-sharing is allowed. This implies h.c.p., as is seen by adding the third c.p. layer. A cubic close-packed structure built of octahedra sharing only vertices is therefore not possible.

One-half of the octahedral sites occupied

S.8. The two simplest arrangements of one-half of the octahedral sites between a pair of c.p. layers are those of the small filled circles in Fig. 35(a) and (b). We consider first the structures resulting from the arrangement (a) between each successive pair of c.p. layers.

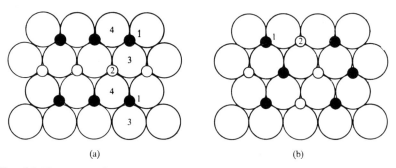

(a)   (b)

FIG. 35. Two ways of selecting one-half of the octahedral sites between a pair of c.p. layers.

On the upper surface of the c.p. layer place six coloured balls in positions (1) and place the second layer above the first. Check that there are four possible positions for the octahedral atoms above the second c.p. layer, namely, 1' (vertically above 1), 2, 3, and 4.

Investigate the structures corresponding to the sequences 1, 1', 1, 2, 1, 3, and 1, 4, and record

(i) the type of close-packing,
(ii) the nature of the structure (layer or 3D framework),
(iii) the way in which the octahedra are linked by vertex-, edge-, or face-sharing.

Name the structures corresponding to the sequences 1, 2 and 1, 4, and describe the environment of the X atoms in the two structures.

Give examples of compounds crystallizing with these structures.

We shall not deal systematically with the structures resulting from the pattern of sites of Fig. 35(b) but note only one structure. Filling of the sites 1 and 2 of Fig. 35(b) between successive pairs of layers implies h.c.p. If all the metal atoms are of the same kind the structure is the analogue of the rutile structure, and it is interesting that PbO_2 crystallizes with both these structures. If alternate layers of metal atoms are Ni and W the structure is that of $NiWO_4$.

Two-thirds of the octahedral sites occupied

S.9. On a close-packed layer place small spheres in the positions *a*, *b*, etc. as shown by the filled circles in Fig. 36. (The small dotted circles are added to show a larger part of the pattern of octahedral sites than can be accommodated on the portion of c.p. layer used in these models.) Place a second c.p.

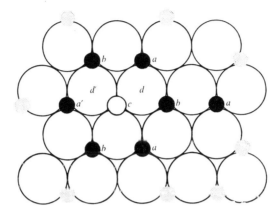

FIG. 36. One-third of the octahedral sites between a pair of c.p. layers.

layer on the first. Investigate the structures resulting from placing the second set of octahedral atoms

    (i) vertically above *a*, *b*, etc.,

    (ii) above the positions *b*, *c*, and then above *c*, *a'*, and so on between successive c.p. layers,

    (iii) above the positions *d*, *d'*.

In each case the pattern of sites occupied at any level should be the same as that of the filled circles *a*, *b*.

    Note the type of close-packing in each model and the sharing of octahedral vertices or faces (in addition to the three edges shared in any horizontal layer). Suggest a reason why the structure (ii) is preferred to (i) or (iii) for the stable form of Al_2O_3 and other sesquioxides. (See also the corundum structure, p. 109.)

All octahedral sites occupied

S.10. If all the octahedral holes in a c.p. assembly of X atoms are occupied by A atoms, the formula of the crystal is AX, and the structures are

                    hexagonal closest packing,   NiAs structure,

                    cubic closest packing,   NaCl structure.

Construct portions of these structures from c.p. X layers. Observe the arrangement of A atoms around an X atom in the NiAs structure and the environment of an A atom. Note the relation of the cubic unit cell of the NaCl structure (containing 4AX) to the c.p. layers, and check that the structure can alternatively be referred to a rhombohedral unit cell containing 1AX.

The description of the NiAs and NaCl structures as c.p. assemblies of X atoms in which A atoms occupy octahedral interstices is not entirely satisfactory. It is true that the immediate neighbours of Ni in NiAs are 6As arranged octahedrally, but there are 2Ni atoms at almost the same distance, and in many intermetallic compounds with this structure these eight neighbours are virtually equidistant from the atom in the octahedral hole. For the NaCl structure the c.p. description is satisfactory only if the metal ion is of the correct size to fit into the X_6 hole leaving the X atoms close-packed. The radius ratios ($r_A : r_X$) for the numerous halides with this structure show that the c.p. picture is physically realistic only for the lithium halides and NaI.

TABLE 6. *Close-packed octahedral structures*

Fraction of octahedral holes occupied	Sequence of c.p. layers		Formula	C.N.s of A and X
	AB ...	*ABC ...*		
All	NiAs	NaCl	AX	6 : 6
2/3	α-Al$_2$O$_3$ LiSbO$_3$	—	A$_2$X$_3$	6 : 4
1/2	*Layer structures* CdI$_2$ *Framework structures* Rutile NiWO$_4$ α-PbO$_2$ α-AlOOH	CdCl$_2$ Atacamite Anatase	AX$_2$	6 : 3
1/3	*Chain structures* ZrI$_3$ *Layer structures* Low-CrCl$_3$ *Framework structures* FeF$_3$	— High-CrCl$_3$ —	AX$_3$	6 : 2
1/4	α-NbI$_4$ (chain)	NbF$_4$ (layer)	AX$_4$	6 : $\frac{2}{1}$
1/5	Nb$_2$Cl$_{10}$ Ru$_4$F$_{20}$ } (molecular)	U$_2$Cl$_{10}$ Mo$_4$F$_{20}$ } (molecular) UF$_5$ (chain)	AX$_5$	6 : $\frac{2}{1}$
1/6	α-WCl$_6$	—	AX$_6$	6 : 1

This point is discussed on p. 74, where it is shown that a similar difficulty arises if the CaF_2 structure is described as a c.p. assembly of Ca^{2+} ions in which F^- ions occupy all the tetrahedral holes. It is nevertheless convenient to include these two AX structures in Table 6 to show their relationship to other c.p. 'octahedral' structures.

STRUCTURES $X_mY_nO_{3m}$ BUILT FROM CLOSE-PACKED XO_3 LAYERS

S.11. We now consider structures built from c.p. layers of atoms of two kinds, X and O, which are present in the ratio 3 : 1. The two simplest layers of this kind in which the X atoms are not adjacent are shown in Fig. 37. (Layers with larger repeat units result from combining strips of these layers.) To form such layers the atoms X and O must have similar sizes. An important difference between the two layers (a) and (b) of Fig. 37 is that it is not possible

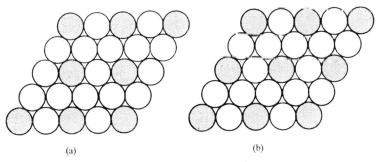

(a)   (b)

FIG. 37. Close-packed XO_3 layers.

to stack (a) layers so as to produce octahedral holes surrounded entirely by O atoms without bringing X atoms into contact, whereas this is possible with the (b) layers. Layers of type (a) are found in intermetallic compounds and in hydroxyhalides (the layer being, for example, $Cl(OH)_3$) where contacts between X atoms are permissible. In complex oxides and halides, on the other hand, the layers are of the type BaO_3 or $CsCl_3$, for example, and contact between Cs^+ or Ba^{2+} ions of adjacent layers would reduce the stability of the structure. In such compounds only (b) layers are found, and we confine our attention here to these two large groups of compounds.

We shall use the symbols A, B, and C for the positions of the c.p. atoms indicated in Fig. 30 (p. 54) and a, b, and c for the corresponding interlayer positions (which are vertically above A, B, and C respectively) for the smaller Y atoms occupying octahedral holes surrounded by six O atoms.

Using two portions of XO_3 layer check
(i) that there is only one arrangement of the layers relative to one another that provides octahedral interlayer positions surrounded entirely by O atoms (O_6 holes) and that there are no X—X contacts;

(ii) that there is one such Y position for every XO_3 in the structure. (Since the number of octahedral holes in a c.p. assembly is equal to the number of spheres, the number of octahedral O_6 holes is equal to one-quarter of the total number of octahedral holes.)

The required relation between a pair of adjacent c.p. layers is that they are related by the translation AB (Fig. 38). This is conveniently arranged in the model by rotating the upper layer through 180° in its own plane and

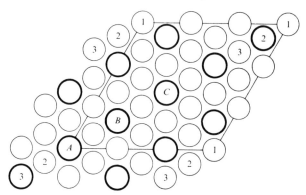

FIG. 38. Structures built from XO_3 layers.

placing it over the first layer so that an X atom falls over B. It will be seen that the X atoms are spaced out in the most symmetrical possible way, A in the lower layer and B in the upper layer, with the small Y atom in the position c (above C).

The formula of a complex oxide (or halide) with this type of structure depends on the fraction of the octahedral holes occupied by Y atoms:

Fraction occupied	Formula
All	XYO_3
$\frac{2}{3}$	$X_3Y_2O_9$
$\frac{1}{2}$	X_2YO_6
etc.	

All the normal c.p. layer sequences are possible, the positions for the inter-layer Y atoms being c between A and B layers, a between B and C, and b between C and A. We may write

$$AcB, \quad BaC, \quad \text{or} \quad CbA,$$

it being understood that the fraction of the a, b, or c holes occupied depends on the formula of the compound as indicated above.

All octahedral O_6 holes occupied

S.12. For the simplest layer sequence, h.c.p., the structure is therefore *AcBc.* ... with all *c* positions occupied in a compound XYO_3.

Stack a number of layers in h.c.p. and insert the Y atoms. The YO_6 octahedra form vertical columns in which each octahedron shares two opposite faces. This is the $CsNiCl_3$ or $BaNiO_3$ structure.

Now stack three layers in c.c.p., the relation between the layers being that shown in Fig. 38, inserting four Y atoms above the second layer. The structure is *AcBaCb* .... Ascertain whether the YO_6 octahedra share vertices, edges,

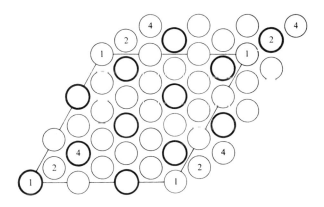

FIG. 39. Layer sequence *hc*.

or faces. In this model the cubic unit cell can be seen with X atoms (blue) at the corners and a Y atom at the body-centre. This is the perovskite structure adopted by many complex oxides and fluorides. (The usual illustration of the structure shows a cell with Y atoms at the corners and X at the body-centre.)

With four c.p. layers construct a portion of the *hc* sequence *AcBcAbCb*, *AcBcAbCb*, ... On the upper surface of the first layer place four Y atoms (small spheres). Place the second c.p. layer (rotated through 180°) in the position indicated by the figures 2 in Fig. 39. The Y atoms above this layer fall vertically above the first four. Now place the third c.p. layer vertically above the first. The fourth c.p. layer is placed with the same orientation as 1 and 3 but translated so that its corner X atom falls above the Y atom marked 4. The Y atoms between the third and fourth c.p. layers then fall above the X atoms of the second layer. The fifth c.p. layer again falls vertically over layers 1 and 3.

Describe the way in which the YO_6 octahedra share vertices, edges, and/or faces.

If sufficient c.p. layers are available more complex layer sequences may be studied, examples of which include:

Symbol	Number of layers in repeat unit	Examples
hhccc	5	$Ba_5Nb_4O_{15}$
hcc	6	$BaTiO_3$ (hexagonal)
ccch	8	$Sr_4Re_2SrO_{12}$
chh	9	$BaRuO_3$
hhcc	12	$Ba_4Re_2MgO_{12}$

(Not all of the octahedral holes are occupied in some of these structures.)

Two-thirds of the O_6 holes occupied

S.13. In some complex halides, of which $Cs_3Tl_2Cl_9$ is an example, two-thirds of the octahedral holes are occupied in a close-packing of alkali metal and halide ions. In the simplest c.p. sequence, h.c.p., the octahedral holes are

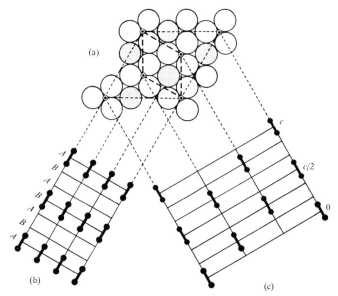

FIG. 40. Crystal structure of $Cs_3Tl_2Cl_9$.

arranged in columns perpendicular to the c.p. layers. By leaving vacant every third octahedral hole in each column, ions $Tl_2Cl_9{}^{3-}$ are formed consisting of two octahedral $TlCl_6$ groups sharing one face. Notice that although the c.p. layer sequence repeats after *two* layers the repeat unit of the structure is now a 6-layer one owing to the arrangement of the metal atoms in the octahedral holes, as may be seen from the elevation of the structure shown in Fig. 40(b). The simplest structure of this kind would be derivable from the $CsNiCl_3$ structure by removing a Y atom at the same height in each column and would

be referable to the unit cell shown by the broken lines in Fig. 40(a). The
$Tl_2Cl_9{}^{3-}$ ions in each column would be at the same heights. In fact the more
uniform distribution of these ions in $Cs_3Tl_2Cl_9$ is that shown in the elevation
of Fig. 40(c).

One-half of the O_6 holes occupied

S.14. Structures in which all the octahedral O_6 holes are occupied between
alternate pairs of c.p. layers have the composition X_2YO_6. All contain discrete octahedral YO_6 ions, and for each c.p. sequence there is a structure of
this kind which corresponds to a XYO_3 structure from which one-half of the
Y atoms have been removed:

C.P. sequence	XYO_3	X_2YO_6
h	$CsNiCl_3$ ($BaNiO_3$)	K_2GeF_6 (Cs_2PuCl_6)
c	$RbCaF_3$	K_2PtCl_6
hc	High-$BaMnO_3$	K_2MnF_6

Construct portions of the K_2GeF_6 and K_2PtCl_6 structures. The latter is
usually referred to a cubic unit cell. If the structure is referred to a hexagonal
cell check that it repeats after six layers.

PERIODIC SPHERE PACKINGS WITH 8- AND 10-COORDINATION

S.15. In the body-centred cubic packing of equal spheres each sphere has
eight equidistant nearest neighbours and six next nearest neighbours at a
slightly greater distance. Assuming the spheres to be rigid and capable of
sliding over one another, imagine this arrangement to be compressed in such
a way that two of the six next nearest neighbours come to the same distance
as the nearest eight, the latter remaining in contact with the central sphere.
We then have a sphere packing in which each sphere is equidistant from ten
others (Fig. 41).

Calculate the distance to the four remaining next nearest neighbours, taking
the diameter of a sphere as unity, and calculate the ratio $c : a$ in the resulting
unit cell.

Sketch the packing in the plane $ABB'A'$ showing the interbond angles
around the central sphere I. How is the packing in the plane $ACC'A'$ related
to that in $ABB'A'$?

The whole infinite assembly can be built up by repetition of the layer of
spheres $ABB'A'$ parallel to itself. Mark on your sketch the positions of the
centres of the spheres of adjacent layers, and use 3S and 7S units held in

the hands to check this point. Note that there is closest packing of the spheres in two perpendicular planes, but in other planes the spheres are not packed in the closest possible way.

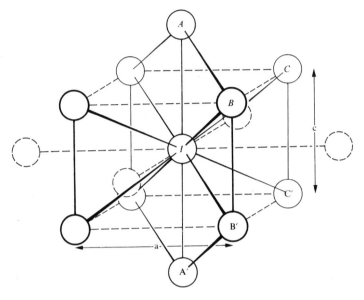

FIG. 41. A sphere-packing with 10-coordination.

If c.p. layers are packed so as to give the lowest possible density of the resulting sphere packing, what is the name of the packing and the number of, and distance to, the nearest and next nearest neighbours? Calculate the density of this packing, defined as the (decimal) fraction of the space which is occupied by the spheres themselves.

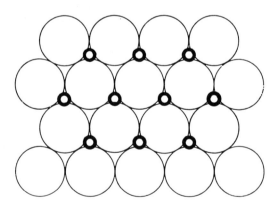

FIG. 42. Positions of metal atoms in MoS_2 layer.

This type of packing of two adjacent layers of spheres can occur if a metal atom forms six bonds directed towards the vertices of a trigonal prism, for the interstices between two layers are surrounded by six spheres arranged in this way. Crystals of one form of MoS_2 are built of double layers of this kind, the metal atoms occupying the positions of the smaller circles in Fig. 42 midway between the layers. Such composite layers can then pack so that there is closest packing between adjacent layers of S atoms of different MoS_2 layers.

With how many S atoms is any S atom in contact in an ideal structure of this kind?

SOME NON-CRYSTALLOGRAPHIC SPHERE PACKINGS

*S.16. We describe here some sphere-packings that are either non-periodic or are periodic in one or two dimensions only. Two 3S units can be placed

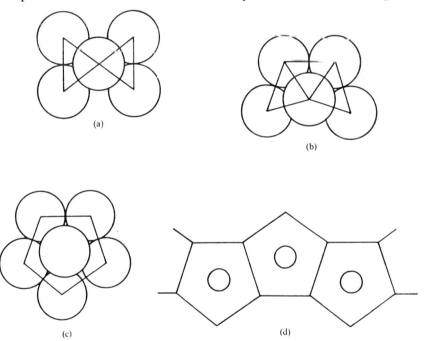

(a)

(b)

(c)   (d)

FIG. 43. Non-periodic sphere-packings (see text).

together in a number of ways which can be studied by holding one unit lightly with the fingers of each hand and placing the units in contact. Count the number of sphere–sphere contacts, which is equal to the number of edges of the polyhedron outlined by their centres. For example, for the octahedral arrangement there are twelve contacts, each sphere being in contact with four others.

Now arrange that one sphere of each unit touches three of the other unit so that two tetrahedral groups are formed. Call these spheres A and A'. There are two extreme configurations which correspond to the two tetrahedra (a) sharing one edge and (b) rotated about the shared edge until a third tetrahedral group is formed between them. When viewed along the direction AA' these appear as shown in Fig. 43(a) and (b). Count the numbers of contacts in (a) and (b) for the individual spheres and record the totals. These numbers give some indication of the compactness of the packing of the six spheres.

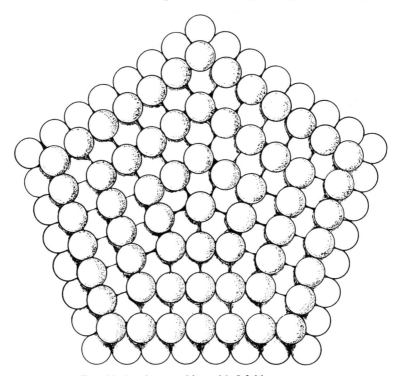

FIG. 44. A sphere-packing with 5-fold symmetry.

The arrangement (b) leads to an interesting sphere-packing. Addition of further 3S units, each related to the previous one in the same way as the two in (b), gives a linear helical structure corresponding to a chain of tetrahedra each sharing two faces. It is not periodic, and the density of packing decreases if further spheres are added to form additional helices surrounding the three composing the original chain.

The grouping (b) is also related to a rather dense sphere packing which is periodic in two dimensions only. In the pentagonal unit of Fig. 11(c) the blue sphere (B) rests in contact with five others forming a regular pentagonal group. A sphere B' in a similar position on the other side of the ring does not touch B, but if we imagine that B and B' are made to touch at least one contact in the 5-ring must be lost (Fig. 43(c)). This unit is (b) plus one additional sphere. This type of packing can continue indefinitely in a direction perpendicular to the plane of the paper, and similar chains may share spheres on two sides to form the puckered layer of Fig. 43(d).

*S.17. In contrast to this 2D sphere-packing there is an interesting 3D packing which possesses a unique 5-fold axis of symmetry. In one layer spheres are arranged to form a series of concentric pentagons with odd numbers of spheres along each side. In contact with this layer is placed a second one in which the concentric pentagons have even numbers of spheres along their sides. By placing the two layers together in intimate contact with their 5-fold axes coincident there results a composite layer (Fig. 44) which can be extended

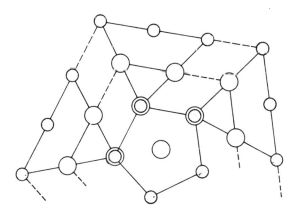

FIG. 45. Construction of model of sphere-packing of Fig. 44.

indefinitely in two dimensions. These composite layers may then be stacked on one another, with their 5-fold axes coincident, to form an infinite packing along the 5-fold axis.

This infinite sphere-packing, which is periodic in one dimension only (along the 5-fold axis), may alternatively be described as consisting of a series of concentric pentagonal bipyramidal shells. Each face of each shell is an equi-lateral triangle of close-packed spheres. A model illustrating this packing can be constructed from the pentagonal unit shown at the right of Fig. 11(c) together with five triangular groups of six c.p. spheres. It is important to note the relation of these to the central group (Fig. 45). One atom of each c.p. layer rests on one of the spheres of the central pentagon, and all the shaded spheres are coplanar. The density of this packing (0·7236) is only slightly lower than that of closest packing (0·7405) and appreciably higher than that of body-centred cubic (0·6802) or radiating icosahedral packing (0·6882).

THE PACKING OF SPHERES OF DIFFERENT SIZES

S.18. We have encountered two special types of structure of this kind, namely, those in which atoms (A) occupy tetrahedral or octahedral holes in assemblies of close-packed (X) atoms. The radii of atoms which would exactly fit the two types of hole are: tetrahedral, 0·225, octahedral, 0·414, if the radius of X is unity. The ratio of the radius of the smaller atom A to that of the X atoms surrounding it is called the radius ratio, $r_A : r_X$. The radius ratios for a number of coordination polyhedra are listed in Table 7. They are the minimum values corresponding to the stability of a particular arrangement of neighbours, for if the radius ratio is less than the value quoted the central A atom (ion) is no longer in contact with all its X neighbours.

TABLE 7. *Radius ratios*

Coordination number	Polyhedron	Minimum radius ratio
4	Tetrahedron	0·225
6	Octahedron	0·414
8	Antiprism	0·645
8	Bisdisphenoid	0·668
8	Cube	0·732
9	Tricapped trigonal prism	0·732
12	Icosahedron	0·902
12	Cuboctahedron	1·000

We might expect that in the absence of directed bonds the numbers of atoms of one kind surrounding another in a crystal consisting of atoms of several kinds would be related to the various radius ratios. This concept is of considerable value in discussions of the structures of complex ionic crystals and also in some groups of intermetallic compounds, but the coordination numbers of ions in some of the simplest structures, for example, the sodium chloride, caesium chloride, fluorite, and antifluorite structures, are not related in any simple way to the relevant radius ratios. For alkali halides with the sodium chloride structure radius ratios range from 0·28 (LiI) to unity (KF), and for crystals with the fluorite structure there is a similar range of values. For K^+ in KCl and for Ca^{2+} in CaF_2 the value of the radius ratio is 0·73. The following simple experiment shows that a maximum coordination number of 9 is possible if the only criterion is the number of larger ions that can be packed around one of the smaller ions.

The largest solid plastic sphere provided has a radius approximately 0·73 times that of the hollow spheres. Place the solid sphere on a group (3S) of three hollow spheres, and in contact with the solid sphere hold a second group 3S with the centres of the spheres vertically above those of the first group. The six spheres outline a trigonal prism. Confirm that a single sphere may be held in contact with the central sphere and also with four spheres forming a rectangular (vertical) face of the prism. Since two more spheres could be placed in similar positions beyond the centres of the other two rectangular faces of the prism, nine spheres of unit radius may be arranged in contact with a central sphere of radius 0·73.

The radius ratio criterion obviously cannot distinguish between cubic 8-coordination and this type of 9-coordination. The former is found in CaF_2 but only 6-coordination of K^+ in KCl, though higher coordination numbers (8, 9, 10, and 12) are found in complex halides.

The positions of the Na^+ (or Cl^-) ions in NaCl and of the Ca^{2+} ions in CaF_2 are those of cubic close-packing, so that as regards the coordinates of the ions these structures may be described in the following way: NaCl, c.c.p. Cl^- ions with Na^+ ions occupying all the octahedral holes; CaF_2, c.c.p. Ca^{2+} ions with F^- ions occupying all the tetrahedral holes. However, the Cl^- ions are in contact in only one of the alkali chlorides, LiCl:

	LiCl	NaCl	KCl	RbCl
Cl–Cl	3·63	3·98	4·45	4·65 Å.

In CaF_2 the Ca–Ca separation of 3·8 Å (radius of Ca^{2+}, 1·00 Å) and the F–F distance, 2·7 Å (radius of F^-, 1·35 Å) show that in fact the F^- ions are in contact, not the Ca^{2+} ions. The structure is therefore preferably described as a simple cubic arrangement of F^- ions in which Ca^{2+} ions occupy one-half of the cubic holes or, alternatively, the CsCl structure from which one-half of the metal ions are missing. The choice of cubic holes occupied is such as to give a tetrahedral arrangement of $4Ca^{2+}$ around F^-. The c.p. description is more realistic for Li_2O (antifluorite structure), though even in this structure the separation of the oxygen ions (3·28 Å) indicates a considerable distortion of closest packing.

The following radii (for c.n. 6) are intended as a rough guide to the relative sizes of some ions.

0·50	0·60	0·70	0·75	0·95	1·00	1·15	1·20	Å
Al^{3+}	Ti^{4+}	Li^+	Zn^{2+}	Cd^{2+}	Na^+	Sr^{2+}	Pb^{2+}	
		Mg^{2+}			Ca^{2+}			

1·35	1·40	1·50	1·70	1·80	1·85	1·95	Å
K^+, F^-	O^{2-}	Rb^+	Cs^+	Cl^-	S^{2-}	Br^-	
Ba^{2+}		OH^-					

$3d$ ions: M^{2+}, $0·75 \pm 0·10$; M^{3+}, $0·60 \pm 0·05$ Å.

4. Structures built from Tetrahedra

CONFIGURATIONS OF A_2X_7 IONS

T.1. THERE is an indefinitely large number of configurations of an A_2X_7 molecule or ion which consists of two tetrahedral AX_4 groups having a common vertex (X atom). The relation between the two tetrahedra is determined by (i) the interbond angle A—X—A at the shared X atom and (ii) the rotation of the tetrahedra relative to one another (the A—X—A angle being fixed).

(i) Angle A—X—A 180°.

The situation is essentially similar to that in C_2H_6 or $N_2H_6{}^{2+}$. There are two extreme configurations, the eclipsed and staggered. One 3-fold symmetry axis of the tetrahedra is retained. Determine the symmetry of the two forms.

(ii) Angle A—X—A less than 180°.

Join two tetrahedra with a flexible 2-connector and hold them (using both hands) with an upper face of each horizontal, the fourth vertex of each in contact with the table, and the plane containing these vertices and the shared vertex vertical. This is the configuration of Fig. 46(a). Keeping the left-hand

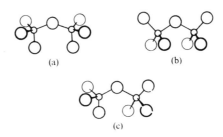

(a)   (b)

(c)

FIG. 46. Configurations of A_2X_7 molecules (ions).

tetrahedron fixed and the upper faces of the tetrahedra coplanar, rotate the other tetrahedron about the shared vertex through 60°. Only two of the edges of the upper faces are now collinear instead of both pairs as previously. This is the configuration (b). Record the symmetry of (a) and (b) and calculate the angle A—X—A for the two configurations.

The configuration (c) is readily derived from the staggered configuration with collinear A—X—A bonds by bending about the bridging X atom; (b) is derived in a similar way from the eclipsed configuration. Record the symmetry of (c).

The following compounds provide examples of ions or molecules with the configurations (a), (b), and (c):

(a) $Zn_4(OH)_2Si_2O_7.H_2O$,

(b) $Rb_2Cr_2O_7$, $NH(SO_3K)_2$, $CH_2(SO_3K)_2$, $K_2S_2O_7$,

(c) Cl_2O_7 (gas).

In (b) the angle A—X—A is larger than $109\frac{1}{2}°$, for example, $116°$ in rubidium dichromate and $136°$ in $SrCr_2O_7$. Both forms (a) and (b) are found in crystals of the latter compound.

Two (finite) molecules formed from tetrahedra, S_3O_9 and P_4O_{10}, have been described in the section on closest packing of equal spheres (p. 57).

For a more general discussion of the geometrical limitations on the value of the angle A—X—A due to the size of the X atoms see the next exercise (*T.2).

INTERBOND ANGLES AT SHARED X ATOMS

*T.2. The interbond angle A—X—A at a vertex (X atom) shared between two polyhedra is of interest because it reflects the nature of the A—X bonds. Because atoms have size there are certain purely geometrical limitations on the values of this angle which are relevant to discussions of the structures of, for example, pyro- and meta-ions.

Assuming that the distance between X atoms of different polyhedra may not be less than X—X within a polyhedron (i.e. the edge length) calculate the permissible values or ranges of values of the angle A—X—A for the cases:

   (i) two tetrahedra sharing a vertex, edge, or face,

   (ii) two octahedra sharing a vertex, edge, or face.

INFINITE PERIODIC STRUCTURES BUILT FROM TETRAHEDRA

Systems built from tetrahedral AX_4 groups may be finite or infinite in one, two, or three dimensions, and they may be neutral molecules or complex ions. Since face-sharing does not occur, the two major classes arise when (a) vertices are common to two tetrahedra or (b) edges are common to two tetrahedra. With regard to the sharing of X atoms between AX_4 tetrahedra the convention adopted is that if an edge is shared its vertices are not counted as shared vertices. In the majority of crystals all tetrahedra are topologically equivalent, that is, each shares the same number of vertices and/or edges in the same way, but we shall note several structures in which this is not so. Examples will also be given of some more complex structures in which each vertex is common to *three* tetrahedra or there is sharing of vertices *and* edges in the same structure.

Vertices common to two tetrahedra

T.3. *Two vertices shared*

Construct two systems in which each tetrahedron shares two vertices. Note their formulae and give examples of molecules or ions with these structures. All results in this section may be checked against Table 14 (p. 142).

'Hybrid' systems, in which some tetrahedra share two vertices and others only one vertex, include poly-ions formed by P, S, and Cr, with X : A ratios between the values $3\frac{1}{2}$ and 3 (for example, $S_3O_{10}^{2-}$ and $P_4O_{13}^{6-}$).

T.4. *Three vertices shared*

Now study the sharing of three vertices of each tetrahedron. A systematic approach is advisable, considering in turn the linking of the tetrahedra first into rings of 3, 4, etc. List the main groups of structures and construct models representing at least two atomic arrangements found in molecules or crystals.

Hybrid systems, in which some tetrahedra share two and others three vertices, have X : A ratios lying between the values 3 and $2\frac{1}{2}$. They are derivable by adding tetrahedra sharing *two* vertices along the links of any 3-connected net at the points of which tetrahedra sharing *three* vertices have been placed.

Construct a portion of the double chain formed in this way from the simple linear system of Fig. 47, placing the additional tetrahedra at the points

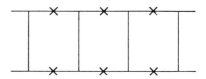

FIG. 47. Infinite double chain (diagrammatic).

indicated. What is the composition of this chain if it is built from SiO_4 tetrahedra, and in which group of silicates is it found? Such double chains may also be regarded as formed from single AX_3 chains by cross-linking at intervals. What is the composition of the double chain if the single chains are cross-linked at every third tetrahedron?

T.5. *Four vertices shared*

If all four vertices of each tetrahedron are shared the basic framework is a 4-connected system, and as in the case of 3-connected systems these include polyhedra, 1-, 2-, and 3-dimensional nets. However, for purely geometrical reasons polyhedral groups of tetrahedra sharing four vertices are not possible.

Show that a linear system of tetrahedra sharing four vertices can be constructed and sketch the 4-connected net on which it is based.

Construct a portion of a layer in which every tetrahedron shares each vertex with one other tetrahedron and all the A atoms lie in one plane. Make a sketch and give examples of compounds with this type of layer structure. Note the A—X—A interbond angle.

Observe that there is a closely related 'puckered' layer. As regards the A—X—A angle how does this layer differ from the 'coplanar' one?

Construct two portions of the *simplest* layer in which each tetrahedron shares three vertices and all the unshared vertices lie to the same side of the layer. Such layers may be joined together to form a double layer within which

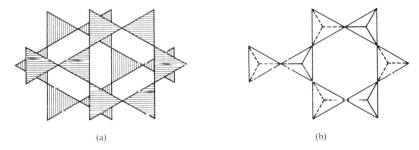

(a)   (b)

FIG. 48. The cristobalite and tridymite structures (see text).

all vertices of each tetrahedron are shared. If constructed from SiO_4 tetrahedra the double layer would be neutral and have the composition SiO_2, but replacement of some Si by Al atoms produces an anion. Give an example of a crystal containing such double-layer ions.

Three-dimensional AX_2 structures formed from tetrahedral AX_4 groups linked by sharing all their vertices arise by placing the groups at the points of 3D 4-connected nets. The simplest structure of this kind therefore arises from the diamond net. It represents the idealized structure of cristobalite (SiO_2). Small portions of this structure and of the closely related structure of tridymite, a second polymorph of SiO_2, may be built in the following way.

T.6. Join tetrahedra at their vertices through 2-connectors maintaining the staggered relationship between each pair. The smallest resulting circuit is a ring of six tetrahedra having one face (three vertices) of each lying in the plane of the ring and the fourth vertex of each alternately above and below this plane. Add a seventh tetrahedron in the same layer. Two such groups of seven tetrahedra can be joined in two ways (Fig. 48), maintaining (a) the staggered or (b) the eclipsed relationship between each pair of tetrahedra so joined. In case (b) there is a horizontal plane of symmetry. These models represent portions of the cristobalite and tridymite structures, idealized in the sense that the A—X—A bond angles have been made equal to 180° instead of values around 140° found in the actual crystals.

T.7. *The cuprite and related structures*

Join together ten tetrahedra with the staggered relationship at each link to form a closed polyhedral grouping bounded by four hexagonal faces (rings). The centres of the tetrahedra are at positions corresponding to the diamond net. Place the model on the table so that it rests on the three tetrahedron vertices projecting from one of the 6-rings. Now build a portion of a second similar framework starting with a tetrahedron at the centre of the truncated tetrahedron, and arrange that there is maximum separation of the tetrahedra of the two nets. This portion of a model of two interpenetrating diamond nets of vertex-sharing tetrahedra illustrates the structures of a number of compounds.

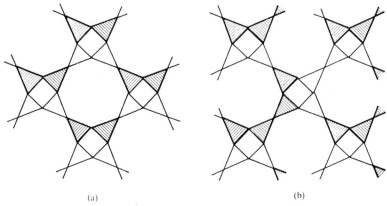

(a)   (b)

FIG. 49. Layers of tetrahedra for 3D aluminosilicates.

(i) If there is an oxygen atom at the centre of each tetrahedron of each net and copper atoms at all the vertices the structure represents two identical interpenetrating nets of composition Cu_2O. This remarkable structure is also adopted by Ag_2O.

*(ii) In this structure the vertices of the tetrahedra (of both nets) occupy the positions of cubic closest packing. If the *tetrahedra* of one net are replaced by *single atoms* A situated at their centres and the second net is built of atoms B situated at all tetrahedral *vertices*, what is the composition of the structure?

What is the arrangement of the B atoms around the larger A atoms? Calculate the distances A–B and A–A and the radius ratio $r_A : r_B$, taking the radius of a B atom as unity.

T.8. *Felspars and related aluminosilicates*

Join together sixteen tetrahedra by sharing three vertices of each to form the portion of layer shown in Fig. 49(a). Use 2-connectors. The centres of the tetrahedra are at the points of one of the simpler 3-connected plane nets (p. 12) having 4-gon and 8-gon circuits. The unshared vertices of the tetrahedra distinguished as shaded triangles in Fig. 49(a) point to one side of the layer and those of the remainder (unshaded triangles) point to the other side. Make a second layer identical to the first. If one of the layers is turned over the two layers can be joined together so that they are related by a plane of symmetry parallel to the layers and midway between them. The structure will obviously repeat indefinitely to form a 3D framework.

The model corresponding to Fig. 49(a) represents the structure of the minerals paracelsian, $Ba(Al_2Si_2O_8)$, and danburite, $Ca(B_2Si_2O_8)$. There is an indefinitely large number of more complex layers, of which Fig. 49(b) is an example. In this layer the arrangement of upward- and downward-pointing tetrahedra implies a larger repeat unit of the pattern. Two layers, each of twenty tetrahedra, may be joined if related by a plane of symmetry. The corresponding 3D framework represents the idealized structure of the felspars, the largest group of rock-forming minerals, which include orthoclase, $KAlSi_3O_8$, albite, $NaAlSi_3O_8$, anorthite, $CaAl_2Si_2O_8$, celsian, $BaAl_2Si_2O_8$, and many minerals of intermediate composition. The detailed configuration of the framework in these aluminosilicates depends on the types of alkali and alkaline-earth ions and on the way in which the Al and Si atoms are distributed in the tetrahedral groups forming the framework.

T.9. Zeolites

There are several types of zeolite structure. In one there are large poly-hedral cavities connected through shared polyhedral faces to form tunnels running in three mutually perpendicular directions. In another group of zeolites there are rather closely knit chains formed from $(Si,Al)O_4$ tetrahedra which are cross-linked at relatively few points, so that there are tunnels parallel to one direction giving the crystal a marked fibrous character. We describe now the structure of one fibrous zeolite.

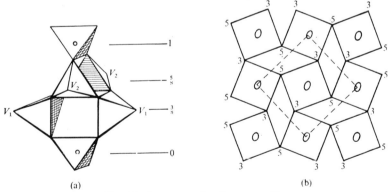

(a)   (b)

FIG. 50. Structure of a fibrous zeolite.

Construct four identical portions of the chain shown in Fig. 50(a), each consisting of six tetrahedra. The heights of the projecting X atoms are three-eighths and five-eighths of the repeat distance along the chain measured from an A atom. (Calculate these fractions precisely from the geometry of the chain, assuming regular tetrahedra.) A chain may conveniently be represented by the diagrammatic end-on view used in Fig. 50(b), from which a portion of the structure may be built. For rigidity complete two 'vertical' 8-membered rings on one side of the model.

Note the concentration of small (4-membered) rings in the chains and the large (8-membered) rings around the tunnels in the structure. This model represents the $(Si,Al)O_2$ framework in the mineral edingtonite, $Ba(Al_2Si_3O_{10}).4H_2O$, no distinction being made between Si and Al atoms. The Ba^{2+} ions and water molecules, which are accommodated in the tunnels, are omitted.

If sufficient tetrahedra are available models may be constructed of the sodalite (ultramarine), the Linde A, and other more complex aluminosilicate frameworks.

Vertices common to three tetrahedra

T.10. Place on the table a number of tetrahedra, each resting on a face, and arrange them to form part of an infinite repeating pattern in which each of three vertices is shared with two other tetrahedra, the fourth being unshared.

What is the formula of this system (a) when built of tetrahedral AX_4 groups or (b) if the shared vertices are X atoms and the unshared ones Y atoms?

Since all the shared vertices lie in one plane and all the unshared vertices are on the same side of this plane, each unshared vertex is equidistant from six others at a distance equal to the length of the tetrahedron edge. This would lead to considerable repulsive forces, particularly if the atoms at the unshared vertices are larger than those at the shared vertices. For example, in crystalline AlOCl every Al atom is surrounded tetrahedrally by 3O and 1Cl, and the Cl atoms are at the unshared vertices of the tetrahedral coordination groups. The repulsions between the Y atoms are greatly reduced if some of the tetrahedra are inverted.

From how many unshared vertices is each unshared vertex equidistant if one-half of the tetrahedra are inverted?

Construct portions of two layers in which one-half of the tetrahedra are pointing to each side of the plane containing the shared vertices and compare with Fig. 106 (p. 141).

Compare the arrangement of the A atoms relative to an X atom (shared vertex) in these layers with that in the layer in which all unshared vertices lie to the same side of the layer.

Tetrahedra sharing edges

T.11. Join two tetrahedra at a common edge. This model represents the structure of a dimeric molecule such as Al_2Cl_6 or Fe_2Cl_6 in the vapour state at low temperatures or of Al_2Br_6 in the crystalline state.

If two opposite edges of every tetrahedron are shared an infinite chain of composition $(AX_2)_n$ is formed. Give examples of crystals built of chains of this kind.

Make two short portions of such a chain with three or four tetrahedra in each, using adjacent arms of 4-connectors to make the junctions. These chains may then be joined laterally by further edge-sharing to give the double chain of composition A_2X_3 shown as the shaded portion of Fig. 51. In this double

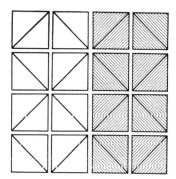

FIG. 51. Tetrahedra sharing three edges to form a double chain (shaded) or four edges to form a layer.

chain three edges of each tetrahedron are shared. It is not known as the structure of a neutral molecule, but represents the form of the complex anion in a number of complex halides including $CsCu_2Cl_3$ and $CsAg_2I_3$.

Further edge-sharing leads to the layer of Fig. 51 in which four edges of each tetrahedron are shared. What is the composition of this layer? Describe the arrangement of bonds from an X atom, and give examples of crystalline compounds built of layers of this type.

If layers of this kind are stacked vertically above one another a 3D structure is formed in which each tetrahedron shares all six edges. Record
  (i) the coordination group around an X atom,
  (ii) the type of packing of the X atoms,
  (iii) the formula and name of the structure, giving examples of compounds crystallizing in this way.

T.12. Join three tetrahedra with a 3-connector and arrange them with one face of each resting on the table. A fourth tetrahedron may be linked to these three by three 2-connectors, as shown by the heavy lines in Fig. 52, so that it shares the edges shown as broken lines with the original tetrahedra. This arrangement of tetrahedra could be extended indefinitely in the plane of the table and would correspond to two layers of c.p. atoms between which all tetrahedral holes are occupied. Note the number and arrangement of A atoms to which each X atom is bonded and hence the formula of the layer.

A fifth tetrahedron (dotted lines) would continue this structure, its fourth vertex pointing upwards. As noted earlier (p. 59) this layer structure is not known. Now rotate this tetrahedron through 180° about the edge *dd*. Its fourth vertex now lies below the position *e*. The four tetrahedra *A*, *B*, *C*, and *D* are now arranged as in the LiOH (OPb) structure, their X atoms being in the

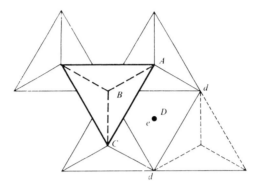

Fig. 52. Relation of LiOH layer to c.p. layers of OH groups (see text).

positions of cubic close-packing. The A atoms at the centres of these four tetrahedra are coplanar, and the LiOH layer may be extended in this plane, which is inclined to the planes of c.p. X atoms at an angle of 54°44′. In the LiOH layer each tetrahedral $Li(OH)_4$ group shares *four* edges and the nearest neighbours of OH are 4Li all lying to one side. This layer gives the maximum separation of the four Li atoms if four (edge-sharing) tetrahedra are to meet at each vertex.

There is the same angular relation between the plane of the HgI_2 layer (p. 59) and the planes of c.c.p. I atoms.

Tetrahedra sharing vertices and edges

T.13. There are very few crystal structures in which tetrahedral coordination groups share edges *and* vertices.

In the simple chain of Fig. 53 each tetrahedron shares one edge and two vertices. It is not known as a discrete structural unit in any crystal, but it has

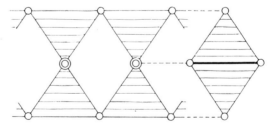

Fig. 53. Chain formed from tetrahedra sharing one edge and two vertices; end-on view at right.

several points of interest. The X atoms are situated not only at the vertices of pairs of edge-sharing tetrahedra but also at the vertices of a chain of octahedra sharing two opposite edges. The chain is therefore very closely related to the 'rutile' chain which is considered in more detail under 'Structures built from octahedra'.

A strip of this chain containing eight tetrahedra may be rolled up to form a cubical unit which is in fact a unit cell of cubic close-packing (see p. 130 for alternative cells). The X atoms are situated at the body-centre and at the mid-points of the edges of a cube, and the model (made with 2-connectors

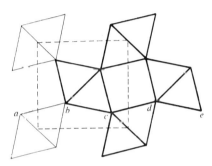

FIG. 54. Projection of the structure of the high-temperature form of BeO.

throughout) provides a useful illustration of c.c.p. Halves of six octahedral holes are visible.

Construct four portions of the chain of Fig. 53 each consisting of four tetrahedra, using opposite arms of 4-connectors at each edge or vertex junction. These chains may be linked to form the portion of the 3D structure shown in plan in Fig. 54 and outlined by heavier lines. (The model is made more rigid by adding four more tetrahedra in obvious places.) Now view the model along the direction of the 'chains' and note that the X atoms are in positions approximating to hexagonal closest packing, *abcde* being the plane of a c.p. layer. Note the close relation of this structure to the wurtzite structure. This model represents the structure of the high-temperature form of BeO, the low-temperature form of which has the wurtzite structure.

*T.14. It is possible to envisage numerous structures built from tetrahedra sharing two vertices and one edge. An edge-sharing pair of tetrahedra may be regarded as a 4-connected unit, having four vertices available for sharing with other similar groups in addition to those belonging to the shared edges (Fig. 55(a)). If such pairs are linked into plane layers, what is the composition of the layer? Portions of two such layers are shown in Fig. 55(b) and (c). If such layers are superposed vertically above one another and joined through the X atoms at the ends of shared edges, 3D structures are formed. What is the composition of such a structure?

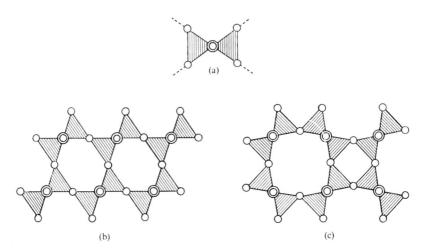

(a)

(b)   (c)

FIG. 55. Formation of layers from tetrahedra sharing one edge and two vertices.

Examples of compounds crystallizing with this type of structure are not yet known.

5. Structures built from Octahedra

OCTAHEDRA may be joined together by sharing vertices and/or edges and/or faces to form an indefinitely large number of structures, finite or infinite in one, two, or three dimensions. We consider first some finite groups of octahedra and then examine more systematically the major families of periodic octahedral structures.

FINITE GROUPS OF OCTAHEDRA

Twelve finite groups built from octahedra are illustrated in Fig. 56, of which the simplest are the dimeric molecules (ions) formed from two octahedral AX_6 groups sharing one vertex, edge, or face.

O.1. Determine the compositions of the groups of Fig. 56 and give examples of molecules or ions having these structures. Examples should not be confined to complexes in which all the ligands are identical or are single atoms, but may include those incorporating ligands of which two or more atoms are bonded to the central A atom (*chelate* ligands).

List the structures of Fig. 56 in which all octahedra are topologically equivalent, that is, have the same number and arrangement of shared vertices, edges, and/or faces.

*O.2. The elements of the VA and VIA sub-groups form some interesting complex oxy-ions formed from octahedral MO_6 groups.

We shall refer to the 2- and 3-octahedron units of Fig. 11 as O_2 and O_3 units respectively.

Join together two O_3 units to form the grouping of Fig. 57(a), which represents the structure of the $Nb_6O_{19}^{8-}$ ion. The $V_{10}O_{28}^{6-}$ ion (Fig. 57(b)) may be constructed from three O_3 units and one additional octahedron. Regarded simply as assemblies of octahedra these two ions are portions of a simple structure; what is the structure?

It is worth noting that a particular group of octahedra may have quite different appearances when viewed in different directions. For example, both (a) and (b) in Fig. 58 are illustrations of the $Mo_8O_{26}^{4-}$ ion. The $Mo_7O_{24}^{6-}$ ion (Fig. 58(d)) has a closely related structure, six of the octahedra being arranged in the same way as in $Mo_8O_{26}^{4-}$. The portion common to the two ions is the group of six octahedra shown in Fig. 58(c). It will be found that these models can be constructed from various combinations of O_3 and O_2 units or, of course, from separate octahedra.

*O.3. *The* MnMo$_9$O$_{32}$$^{6-}$ *ion*

This grouping of nine MoO$_6$ octahedra around a central MnO$_6$ group is another example of an edge-sharing group of octahedra which may be regarded as a portion of the NaCl structure.

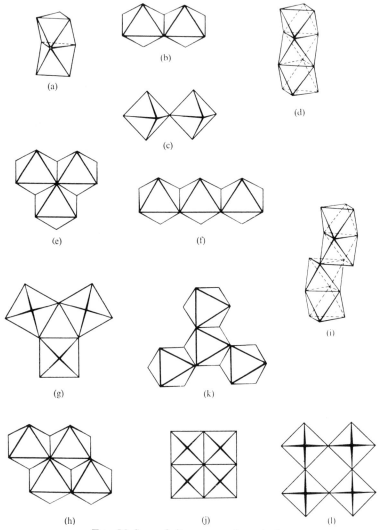

FIG. 56. Some finite groups of octahedra.

It is readily constructed by making first the 'equatorial' group of four coplanar octahedra (using 2-connectors) and then attaching two O$_3$ units arranged as shown in Fig. 59. Six further 2-connectors joining appropriate pairs of vertices are sufficient to make a rigid model.

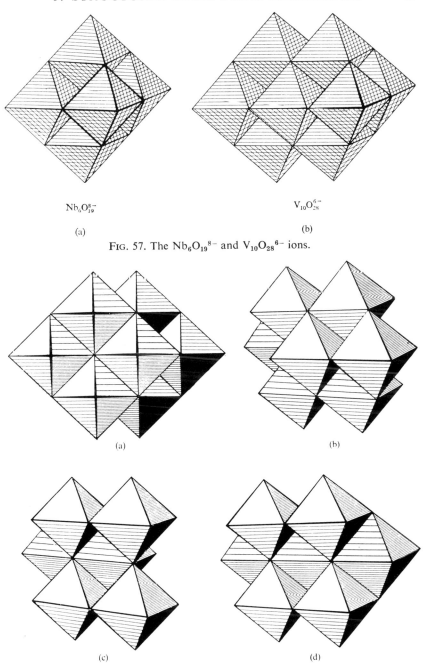

$Nb_6O_{19}^{8-}$

(a)

$V_{10}O_{28}^{6-}$

(b)

FIG. 57. The $Nb_6O_{19}^{8-}$ and $V_{10}O_{28}^{6-}$ ions.

(a)

(b)

(c)

(d)

FIG. 58. (a) and (b) $Mo_8O_{26}^{4-}$ ion, (d) $Mo_7O_{24}^{6-}$ ion, and (c) the portion common to the two ions.

*O.4. *The* $PW_{12}O_{40}{}^{3-}$ *ion*

We investigate first the three most symmetrical ways of joining together four O_3 units to form a polyhedral complex containing twelve A atoms.

(a) Join along the edges A, A', etc. (Fig. 60(a)), the tetrahedral cavities (shaded) facing inwards towards the centre of the unit. Use 3-connectors at A, A', etc. The resulting complex is a cuboctahedral structure with full cubic symmetry.

Of which simple structure is this group a portion?

Sketch the complex when viewed normal to a square face of the cuboctahedron, and insert in Table 8 the number of X atoms (vertices of octahedra), the type of hole at the centre of the complex, and the type of packing of the X atoms.

TABLE 8. *Properties of 12-octahedra complexes*

	(a)	(b)	(c)
Number of X atoms			
Shape of central cavity			
Type of packing of X atoms			

In the next two models the tetrahedral cavities of the O_3 units are on the *outsides* of the models.

(b) Join the four O_3 units by sharing the edges shown as heavy lines in Fig. 60(b), using 2-connectors to form a truncated tetrahedral complex. Make a sketch of the complex to compare with that in (a) and make the appropriate entries in Table 8.

(c) Join the four O_3 units by sharing the vertices BB', CC', and DD' in pairs with other units. Although the A atoms (octahedra centres) are situated at the vertices of a (distorted) cuboctahedron the symmetry is clearly only tetrahedral, for one-half of the triangular groups of octahedra are edge-sharing groups and the others are vertex-sharing groups.

Examine the model, complete Table 8, and consider particularly the mode of packing of the X atoms, which is also described in Experiment **S.3** on the closest packing of spheres. This model, somewhat surprisingly, represents the structure of the 12-heteropoly acid anion in $H_3PW_{12}O_{40}$ and many similar acids and salts.

*O.5. *The* $P_2W_{18}O_{62}{}^{6-}$ *ion*

Join an O_3 unit through vertices BB', etc. (Fig. 60(b)) to three O_2 units using the vertices EE' of the latter (Fig. 60(c)). Make further connections through the vertices GG' to form a ring of six (three edge-sharing pairs of) octahedra

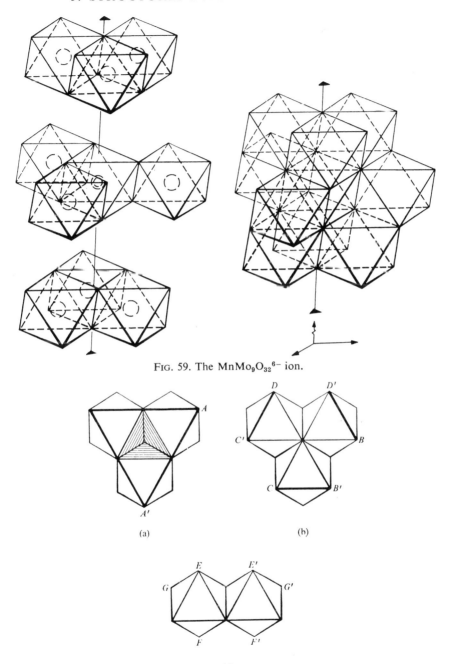

FIG. 59. The $MnMo_9O_{32}^{6-}$ ion.

(a)   (b)

(c)

FIG. 60. Construction of 12-octahedra complexes.

surmounted by the group of three octahedra. This group of nine octahedra is a portion of the $PW_{12}O_{40}^{3-}$ anion. Two such sub-units may be linked through the three pairs of vertices FF' to form a polyhedral grouping of eighteen octahedra. If difficulty is experienced with this model, reference may be made to Fig. 108 (p. 144).

Verify that the composition corresponds to $P_2W_{18}O_{62}^{6-}$ if the model is built of WO_6 octahedra with P atoms located at the centres of the two tetrahedral cavities in the interior.

SYSTEMATIC DERIVATION OF OCTAHEDRAL STRUCTURES

In view of the great number and variety of these structures it is convenient to begin with those in which octahedra share *only* vertices, *only* edges, or *only* faces. With regard to the sharing of X atoms between AX_6 octahedra the convention adopted is that if an edge is shared its two vertices are not counted as shared vertices, and similarly the three edges and three vertices of a shared face are not counted as shared edges or vertices. We shall then consider some of the simpler structures in which octahedra share vertices *and* edges, vertices *and* faces, and finally vertices, edges, *and* faces, for these groups include some important crystal structures (e.g. rutile and corundum).

We have seen that in some quite simple finite groupings the octahedra are not topologically equivalent. For example, the terminal octahedra in any linear edge-sharing system such as that of Fig. 56(f) share only one edge, whereas the intermediate ones share two edges. However, in the infinite linear chain formed by extending such a group in both directions all the octahedra become equivalent. Similarly the unit (h) can be extended to left and right to form a double chain in which all octahedra share four edges, while (k) would form a 2-dimensional pattern in which all octahedra share three edges. Thus the simplest periodic systems are built of octahedra sharing the same numbers (and arrangements) of vertices, edges, and/or faces. It may be assumed that all octahedra are topologically equivalent in the systems we describe unless the contrary is stated.

The non-equivalence of X atoms: the formulae of octahedral structures

Clearly unshared and shared X atoms are not equivalent; the former are attached to one A atom and the latter to two or more A atoms. Since the basis of our classification is the way in which vertices, edges, or faces are shared it is important to understand how the formula of a system of octahedra joined together in a particular way is related to the geometry of the structure.

If two AX_6 octahedra share a vertex the shared X atom is common to two octahedra only. There is therefore a simple relation between the formulae of structures in which octahedra share only vertices and the numbers of shared vertices:

Number of shared vertices	1	2	3	4	(5)	6
Formula	A_2X_{11}	AX_5	A_2X_9	AX_4	(A_2X_7)	AX_3

(The case of five shared vertices will be omitted as highly improbable.)

On the other hand, if two or more edges (faces) are shared the ratio X : A in the formula is *not* simply related to the number of shared edges (faces). This ratio depends on whether the shared edges (faces) have X atoms in

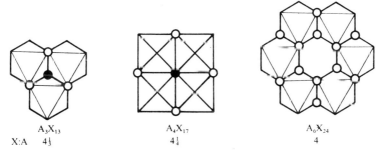

	A_3X_{13}	A_4X_{17}	A_6X_{24}
X:A	$4\frac{1}{3}$	$4\frac{1}{4}$	4

FIG. 61. Finite groups in which octahedra share two edges.

common, for in the resulting structure some X atoms may be common to two and others to three or four octahedra. Fig. 61 shows three groups of octahedra in each of which all the octahedra are topologically equivalent and all share two edges. In the first the central X atom is common to three octahedra, and three others are common to two octahedra. In the second the central X atom belongs to four octahedra and four are common to two octahedra, while in the third grouping twelve of the X atoms are common to two octahedra.

We shall see later that the sharing of four edges can give a double chain of composition AX_3 or (a different set of edges) a layer A_3X_8, and that the formula AX_3 can arise from the sharing of three edges.

The non-equivalence of X atoms is found in many molecules and crystals—a striking example is provided by the structure of MoO_3 (p. 153)—and although it is seldom discussed it would seem to be of considerable chemical interest.

Although there is therefore no simple connection between the formula and the number of shared edges (faces) it is nevertheless convenient to summarize in Table 9 the simpler types of octahedral structure. It must be emphasized that the formulae marked with an asterisk apply only to those structures in which *all shared X atoms belong to the same number of octahedra*.

TABLE 9. *Formulae of simple octahedral structures*

Number shared	Vertices	Edges	Faces	Possible types of complex
1	A_2X_{11}	A_2X_{10}	A_2X_9	Dimers only
2	AX_5	AX_4*	AX_3*	Finite groups, rings, or infinite chains
3	(A_2X_9)	AX_3*		⎫
4	AX_4			Polyhedra, 1-, 2-, and 3-dimensional complexes
6	AX_3	AX_2*		⎭

* Assuming all shared X atoms belong to the same number of octahedra.

Of the structures in Table 9 we may distinguish as a special set those (shown in heavy type) in which *all* X *atoms are equivalent*, i.e. all are shared and each belongs to the same number of octahedra, two in the AX_3 and three in the AX_2 structures. These are the structures in which each octahedron shares

(i) six vertices with six other octahedra,
(ii) the three edges of Fig. 112(e) (p. 148),
(iii) the six edges of Fig. 113(a) or (b) (p. 149), or
(iv) two opposite faces.

We shall see later that (i) and (ii) correspond to families of related structures while (iii) and (iv) produce a single structure in each case.

For reference purposes the main types of octahedral structure are summarized in Table 10, in which the grouping of the structures is that adopted in the following pages.

OCTAHEDRA SHARING VERTICES ONLY

O.6. Join two octahedra to form the dimeric A_2X_{11} group. What is the range of permissible A—X—A bond angles assuming that the closest approach of X atoms of different octahedra is not less than the edge-length of an octahedron? Compare your answer with that on p. 137.

O.7. Make portions of the *simplest possible* structures in which all octahedra share

2 adjacent (*cis*) vertices,
2 opposite (*trans*) vertices,
4 equatorial vertices, or
6 vertices (with six other octahedra).

List the structures with their formulae and give examples of compounds with these structures. Make sketches of the structures.

TABLE 10. Structures built from octahedral AX_6 groups

Vertices only shared

2 AX_5 chain: BiF_5
4 AX_4 layer: SnF_4, K_2NiF_4
6 AX_3 framework: ReO_3, $Sc(OH)_3$
$\qquad FeF_3$, etc.
$\qquad$ Perovskite
$\qquad$ W bronzes

Vertices and faces shared

ABO_3 structures
Hexagonal $BaTiO_3$
High-$BaMnO_3$
$BaRuO_3$

Vertices and edges shared

AX_3, A_3X_8, A_2X_5 layers
$\quad$ (V oxyhydroxides)
AX_2 frameworks

$\qquad$ Rutile structure
$\qquad \alpha$-AlO.OH
$\qquad Eu_3O_4$
$\qquad CaTi_2O_4$
$\qquad \alpha$-MnO_2

$\qquad BeY_2O_4$
AX_3 layer: MoO_3
AX_3 framework: $CaTa_2O_6$

Vertices, edges, and faces shared

α-Al_2O_3 (corundum)
γ-$Cd(OH)_2$

Edges only shared

2 AX_4 chains: NbI_4, $TcCl_4$
3 AX_3 layer: $CrCl_3$, BiI_3
4 AX_3 double chain: NH_4CdCl_3
$\qquad A_3X_8$ layer: Nb_3Cl_8
6 AX_2 layer: CdI_2, $CdCl_2$
$\qquad AX_2$ double layer: $MOCl$, $\gamma'MO.OH$
$\qquad AX_2$ framework: $Cu_2(OH)_3Cl$

Faces only shared

2 AX_3 chain: ZrI_3
$\qquad BaNiO_3$, $CsNiCl_3$

Suggest other types of layer structure that could be formed from octahedra sharing four equatorial vertices and hence other 3D structures for octahedral groups sharing all six vertices. Are structures belonging to these two families known?

O.8. Construct a representative portion of the ReO_3 structure from eight octahedra (Fig. 62(a)). Describe the type of packing of the oxygen atoms, and for further comments on this structure see p. 146.

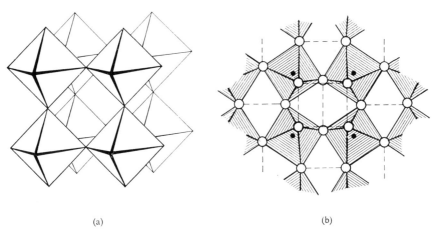

(a)   (b)

FIG. 62. The crystal structures of (a) ReO_3 and (b) $Sc(OH)_3$.

What is the name of the structure similar to the ReO_3 structure but with an additional atom, of a third kind, at the centre of the cubic unit cell? Give examples of compounds with this structure.

If the model of the ReO_3 unit cell is held in both hands it will be found that it can be distorted into the form shown in plan in Fig. 62(b). Why do the shorter O—O contacts between oxygen atoms of different octahedra (broken lines) make this a more suitable structure for compounds such as $Sc(OH)_3$?

*O.9. Devise a layer structure in which each octahedron shares three vertices (with three other octahedra). What is its formula, and which structure would result if the other three vertices of each octahedron are shared to continue the structure in three dimensions?

OCTAHEDRA SHARING EDGES ONLY

O.10. *One edge shared*

Make a dimeric unit A_2X_{10} consisting of two octahedra with a common edge. What are the permissible values of the interbond angle A—X—A assuming that X atoms of different octahedra may not approach closer than in an AX_6 octahedron? Check with p. 137.

O.11. *Two edges shared*

Construct models in which each octahedron shares

(i) two edges with a common vertex,

(ii) two opposite edges.

Determine the formulae and make sketches. Sketch also the end-on view of the chain (ii). We shall refer to this as the 'rutile chain', since the structure of this form of TiO_2 can conveniently be built from sub-units of this kind.

Check that there is a second way of selecting two edges which have no common vertex; this leads to a family of structures which are described in *O.15.

(i)   (ii)   (iii)

FIG. 63. Three ways of selecting four edges of an octahedron.

O.12. *Three edges shared*

Verify that there is only one way of selecting three edges of an octahedron if no two are to have a common vertex. Make a model of a structure in which every octahedron shares these three edges, and suggest other structures of the same general type that could be constructed.

O.13. *Six edges shared*

Verify that there are two ways of selecting six edges so that each vertex is common to two *shared* edges. Make a portion of the structure in which each octahedron, resting on one face, shares the six inclined edges with six other octahedra. Note the formula, and check that each X atom is common to three octahedra. Sketch the arrangement of bonds from an X atom, showing the interbond angles.

For the structure in which the other set of six edges is shared see *O.17.

O.14. *Four edges shared*

(i) Make a model with each octahedron lying on a face and sharing the four edges indicated by the heavy lines in Fig. 63(i). Sketch a portion of the chain and its end-on view, and determine its composition. How many kinds of non-equivalent X atoms are there, and to how many octahedra does each belong? This chain is formed from two rutile chains joined laterally by further edge-sharing, and may be described as the 'double rutile' chain.

(ii) Construct a model with each octahedron resting on one face and sharing the four edges of Fig. 63(ii). Make a sketch and determine the composition.

(iii) Construct a model in which each octahedron shares four edges meeting at one vertex (Fig. 63(iii)).

Give examples of structures of types (i), (ii), and (iii) found in crystals.

Describe the mode of packing of the X atoms in the layers constructed in **O.13**, **O.12**, and **O.14**(ii), and hence suggest alternative descriptions of the layers.

Further examples of structures in which octahedra share only edges

*O.15. *Two edges shared*

We now consider the second way of selecting two edges that have no common vertex.

Relative to a given edge a (Fig. 64) there are four such edges, b, c, d, and e, which are symmetrically equivalent in relation to a on an isolated octahedron.

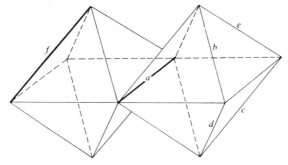

Fig. 64. Octahedra sharing two edges with no common vertex.

However, the configuration of a chain is determined by the choice of pairs of shared edges of *successive* octahedra. If we arbitrarily choose f as the second shared edge of the left-hand octahedron in Fig. 64 then there are four ways of choosing the second shared edge of the adjacent octahedron, giving the combinations *fab*, *fac*, *fad*, and *fae*. The simplest chains arise if we maintain the same relationship between all successive pairs of octahedra, or, in other words, the same arrangement of shared edges relative to any particular shared edge.

Connect together octahedra each sharing two edges so that the edges shared between adjacent octahedra correspond to (i) *fab*, (ii) *fac*, (iii) *fad*, and (iv) *fae*. In order to maintain the maximum possible separation of X atoms of different octahedra (and to define the geometry of the chains) make the group of four atoms

coplanar at each junction.

Sketch the resulting systems and compare with Fig. 114 (p. 149). A planar system may be represented with the octahedra resting on faces. Note that the chain *fac* can also be drawn with the octahedra viewed along a body-diagonal; the chains *fad* and *fae* should also be drawn in this way. Observe that *fad* and *fae* are helical chains. For *fad* calculate the inclination of the screw axis to its projection in the plane of the paper.

Examples of these octahedral systems include

fab: $TeMo_6O_{24}^{6-}$,

fac: $TcCl_4$, $Li(CuCl_3.H_2O).H_2O$,

fad: —

fae: $Na(H_2O)_4$ in $Na_2[SiO_2(OH)_2].8H_2O$.

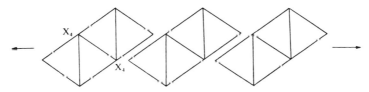

FIG. 65. Corrugated layer formed from octahedra sharing six edges.

O.16. *Six edges shared*

The corrugated layer which is the structural unit in compounds such as γ-AlO.OH and FeOCl provides an example of a third way of selecting six of the twelve edges of an octahedron.

Make three short portions of double rutile chain using 4-connectors at the points marked X_4 in Fig. 65. These connectors will then serve to join appropriate atoms of different chains to form corrugated layers which extend perpendicular to the plane of the paper.

(a) Verify that the arrangement of shared edges is that of Fig. 113(c), p. 149, and

(b) determine the composition of the layer. This is conveniently done by first checking that all the octahedra are equivalent and then finding the number of octahedra to which each X atom belongs.

The atacamite and spinel structures

*O.17. *The atacamite structure*

We referred in **O.13** to a second way of selecting six edges so that each vertex is common to two shared edges. These are the edges of a pair of opposite faces (Fig. 113(b)).

Join three O_3 units by 2- and 3-connectors as indicated in Fig. 66(a), placing each unit with its central tetrahedral cavity uppermost. Within a unit each octahedron shares two edges. By sharing the edges shown as full heavy lines in Fig. 66(a) each octahedron will then share three edges (all belonging to one face) with three other octahedra. Place an octahedron above each of the tetrahedral holes *A*, *B*, and *C*. The edges shown by the heavy broken lines then correspond to the three outer lower edges of an O_3 unit. Attach three

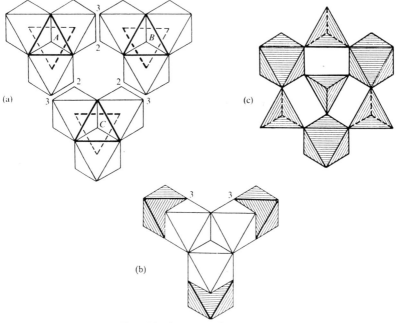

FIG. 66. The atacamite structure.

octahedra to the underside of a fourth O_3 unit as shown in Fig. 66(b) using 3-connectors. This group of six octahedra will rest on (a) with the heavily drawn edges in (a) in common. This portion of structure does not show any octahedron with all its six shared edges, but it will be evident that if the structure is continued every octahedron will in fact share the six edges indicated in Fig. 113(b). The structure can be described either as built from rutile chains or from octahedra arranged in groups of four around tetrahedral holes.

(i) What is the formula corresponding to this structure?

(ii) What is the type of packing of the X atoms, and what are the fractions of octahedral holes occupied between successive pairs of c.p. layers?

(iii) How is the structure related to the NaCl structure?

(iv) How is it related to the diamond structure, and how could it be derived from that structure?

(v) What is the arrangement of A atoms relative to an X atom, and how does this compare with the environment of an X atom in the $CdCl_2$ or CdI_2 layer?

In spite of the simplicity of this structure and its relationship to the $CdCl_2$ structure it is not adopted by any compound AX_2 (for example, dihalide or dihydroxide), but it represents the idealized structure of one polymorph of $Cu_2(OH)_3Cl$, the mineral atacamite.

*O.18. *The spinel structure*

Although there are both tetrahedral and octahedral coordination groups in this structure it is convenient to describe it here because of its close relationship to the previous structure.

A tetrahedral disposition of metal atoms around X atoms results if cations occupy the tetrahedral holes in the central layer (Fig. 66(c)) of the atacamite model. The tetrahedra point alternately up and down, and they may be added to the upper part (b) using the 3-connectors. The whole composite layer (b)–(c), consisting of six octahedra and four tetrahedra, may be linked to the lower layer (a).

Determine the composition if the octahedral holes are occupied by A atoms and all the tetrahedral holes indicated in Fig. 66(c) by B atoms. This is the normal spinel structure of many complex oxides.

What are the values of the interbond angles A—X—A in this structure?

OCTAHEDRA SHARING VERTICES AND EDGES

We now come to the large group of structures in the centre of Table 10, structures in which both vertices and edges of octahedra are shared. It is convenient to regard them as built from infinite chains which are then joined along their lengths by sharing vertices. In the first group of structures the sub-unit is the single rutile chain or a multiple rutile chain.

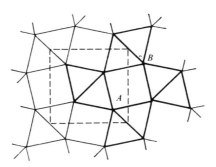

FIG. 67. The rutile structure.

The rutile structure

O.19. Construct four portions of rutile chain, each consisting of two octahedra, using 3-connectors for the edge junctions. Join these chains together to form the part of Fig. 67 drawn with heavy lines.

What is the arrangement of A atoms around an X atom in the most symmetrical form of this structure *built with regular octahedra*?

Examination of this structure will show that there cannot at the same time be the most symmetrical arrangement (regular octahedral) of 6X around A and the most symmetrical arrangement of 3A around X (three coplanar with interbond angles of 120°).

Note also that the structure can be made more compact by rotating the chains so that all the squares in Fig. 67 become rhombuses. This occurs in crystalline CrO.OH (green form) and InO.OH as the result of hydrogen bonding across *AB* (and similar places), that is, between O and OH groups.

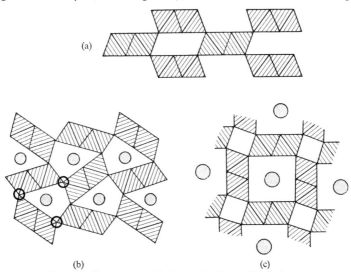

(a)

(b)   (c)

FIG. 68. Structures built from double rutile chains.

*Deduce the content of the unit cell of the rutile structure. Assuming regular octahedra, calculate (i) the axial ratio $c : a$ of the tetragonal unit cell, and (ii) the coordinates of the atoms (as fractions of a and c), placing an A atom at the origin. Insert the coordinates on a plan of the unit cell. (iii) Calculate $c : a$ and the coordinates of the atoms for the form of this structure in which there is an equilateral triangular arrangement of 3Ti around, and coplanar with, each O atom. (Assume tetragonal symmetry.)

Framework structures built from 'double rutile' chains

O.20. We have noted the γ-AlO.OH (layer) structure as resulting from the sharing of additional edges between octahedra of double rutile chains. If double rutile chains are linked by sharing vertices the simplest structures arise when X_1 atoms of one chain are shared with X_2 atoms of other chains. All X atoms are then common to three octahedra. The three framework structures illustrated in Fig. 68 are all of this kind. In (a) the X–X distances across the cavities are similar to those in the AX_6 groups, and the structure is found for compounds such as α-AlO.OH (diaspore). In (b) and (c) the tunnels can accommodate atoms appreciably larger than the A atoms in the octahedral framework, and these structures are adopted by compounds such as CaV_2O_4 and $K_{2-y}Mn_{8-z}O_{16}$ respectively. (In the latter compound the K^+ ions balance the negative charge on the framework which arises from the substitution of some Mn^{4+} by Mn^{2+} ions.)

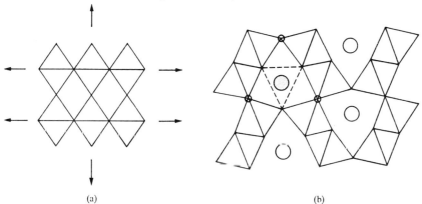

(a)   (b)

FIG. 69. Structures built from (a) single and (b) double rutile chains.

Construct a portion of the CaV_2O_4 structure from four short lengths of the double rutile chain, and determine the arrangement of O atoms around a Ca^{2+} ion (shaded) given that the ion is at the same height above the plane of the paper as the three O atoms shown as small circles.

*O.21. In the rutile structure and in the structures of Fig. 68 built from double rutile chains the X_1 atoms of one chain have been shared with X_2 atoms of neighbouring chains so that all X atoms are common to three octahedra. The alternative way of linking the chains, by sharing pairs of X_1 or X_2 atoms, gives a structure in which some X atoms are common to two and the remainder to four octahedra. The 3D structure of this type built from single rutile chains is not known; it is shown in elevation in Fig. 69(a). Similar structures may be formed from multiple rutile chains, and one of these has been shown to be the structure of $CaTi_2O_4$.

Construct a portion of the structure of Fig. 69(b) from short lengths of double rutile chains.

(a) How many kinds of non-equivalent O atoms are there in this structure? To how many Ti atoms is each bonded?

(b) Sketch the arrangements of Ti atoms around each type of O atom and describe them as completely as possible.

(c) What is the arrangement of O atoms around an atom of Ca (shaded circle) if this is at the same height above the plane of the paper as the three O atoms shown as small circles?

(d) Check the composition of the crystal if Ca atoms occupy all possible positions of this kind.

*O.22. By determining the numbers of octahedral AX_6 groups to which each X belongs deduce the compositions of the layers of Fig. 70 which are built

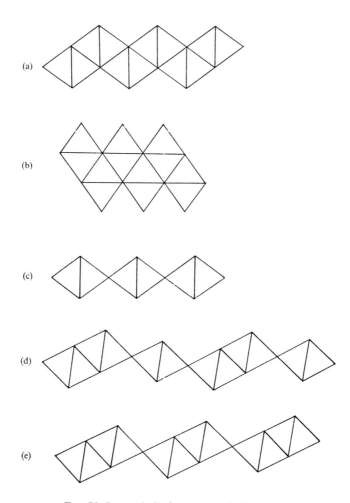

FIG. 70. Layers built from octahedral chains.

from single and/or double rutile chains (chain direction perpendicular to the plane of the paper). Make models if necessary. In (a) and (b) there is sharing of further edges and in (c), (d), and (e) sharing of vertices between chains.

Of what structure is the (unknown) layer (b) a portion if regarded as an assembly of octahedra?

Structures built from 'double ReO_3' chains

O.23. It is convenient to refer to the AX_5 chain of Fig. 71(a) as the ReO_3 chain. The ReO_3 and hexagonal tungsten bronze structures are shown in Fig. 72 viewed in the direction of these chains. We may envisage other groups

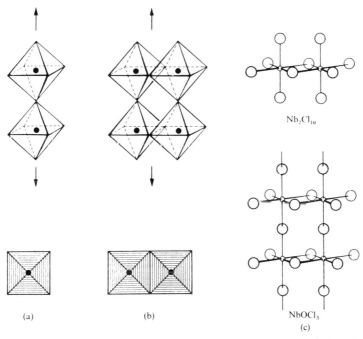

FIG. 71. (a) ReO_3 (AX_5) chain; (b) double ReO_3 (AX_4) chain, and the Nb_2Cl_{10} molecule and $NbOCl_3$ chain molecule.

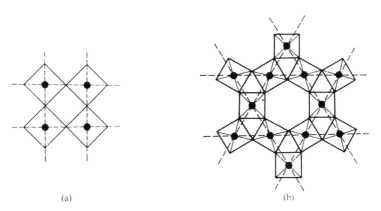

FIG. 72. Projections of (a) ReO_3 and (b) hexagonal tungsten bronze structures viewed in the direction of the 'chains'.

of structures based on 'multiple ReO_3' chains, that is, chains formed by lateral edge-sharing as in Fig. 71(b). The double chain is the structural unit in $NbOCl_3$, the structure of which is related to that of the dimeric Nb_2Cl_{10} molecule in crystalline niobium pentachloride (Fig. 71(c)).

There are three analogues of the ReO_3 structure built from double instead of single ReO_3 chains sharing vertices with four surrounding chains to form 3D structures. One is illustrated in Fig. 73(a); sketch projections of the other two, along the chain direction.

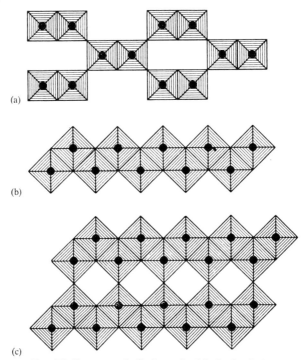

FIG. 73. Structures built from double ReO_3 chains.

O.24. Construct a small portion of the structure of Fig. 73(a) from four short lengths of double ReO_3 chain. What is the composition of the framework if built of octahedral AX_6 groups? The framework is electrically neutral only if the charge on the A ion is three times that on X. For an oxide this implies an ion A^{6+} or for a halide A^{3+}. For ions carrying smaller charges the framework is negatively charged; it is a 3D ion. Cations of a second kind may therefore be accommodated in the interstices giving structures for complex oxides (halides). The perovskite structure (described in **S.12**) is related in this way to the ReO_3 structure, and the hexagonal bronze structure of Fig. 72 provides an example of a more complex structure of this kind built from single ReO_3 chains.

No examples are known of compounds having the very symmetrical structure of Fig. 73(a), but the modified form shown in Fig. 74 represents the crystal structure of $CaTa_2O_6$. The shaded circles represent Ca^{2+} ions, and all atoms drawn as heavy circles are at the same height above the plane of the projection. From the model, distorted into the form of Fig. 74, determine the

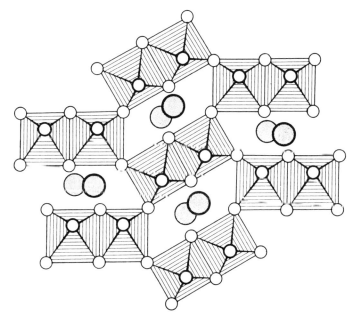

FIG. 74. The structure of $CaTa_2O_6$.

arrangement of O atoms around Ca for the 'ideal' structure built from regular octahedra. In the actual structure, as illustrated, the TaO_6 octahedra are distorted; how does this distortion affect the environment of a calcium ion?

O.25. By further edge-sharing the double ReO_3 chains form the layer of Fig. 73(b). Construct a portion of the layer and determine its composition.

What is the composition of the 3D structure formed if these layers are further linked by sharing their unshared vertices as indicated in Fig. 73(c)?

More complex structures

*O.26. Make four portions of the edge-sharing chain shown in Fig. 75(a) each consisting of four octahedra: 4-connectors should be used, for although 3-connectors would suffice for this portion of a chain 4-connectors would be required in the infinite chain.

What is the composition of the infinite chain?

Join four chains as in Fig. 75(b) using 2-connectors. What is the composition of the resulting 3D framework?

From which structure could this one be derived, and what fractions of A and X atoms would have to be removed?

*O.27. Construct two portions of the same chain, each consisting of six octahedra (three pairs along the chain axis). These units may now be joined

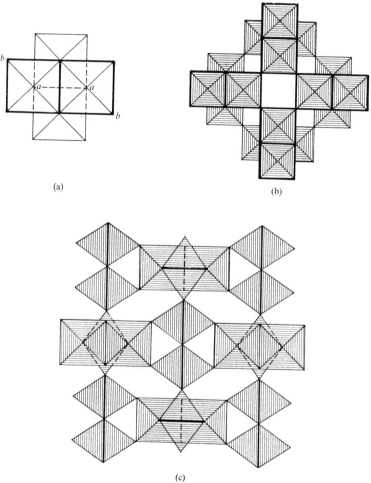

(a)

(b)

(c)

FIG. 75. More complex octahedral structures (see text).

by sharing the vertices of type *a* in Fig. 75(a) to form an infinite chain in which one-third of the octahedra share five edges and two-thirds share three edges and two vertices. These chains may now be joined laterally by sharing the vertices *b* to form a layer.

Determine the composition of the layer. This is most readily done by noting the composition of the 6-octahedron sub-unit and then adjusting to allow for the sharing of vertices *a* and *b*.

*O.28. Construct the model from the plan of Fig. 75(c), given that the structure is built of edge-sharing pairs of octahedra which are linked to form a 3D structure as indicated in the figure.

What is the composition of the framework, and to which of the basic 3D nets is it related?

OCTAHEDRA SHARING FACES ONLY

The sharing of one face of each octahedron leads to the A_2X_9 group illustrated in Fig. 56(a). Ions of this kind are present in salts such as $Cs_3Tl_2Cl_9$, where Tl atoms occupy pairs of adjacent (face-sharing) octahedral interstices between c.p. $CsCl_3$ layers (**S.13**). Sharing of a pair of opposite faces gives an infinite chain of octahedra which represents the form of the molecule in crystalline ZrI_3 and of the complex anion in $CsNiCl_3$ and $BaNiO_3$. These structures have been described as c.p. structures in **S.7** and **S.12** respectively.

OCTAHEDRA SHARING FACES AND VERTICES

O.29. Construct a portion of the hexagonal $BaTiO_3$ structure. Commence with a number of single octahedra resting on the table and correctly spaced to allow for the fact that the model is being built from TiO_6 octahedra, that is, the Ba^{2+} ions are omitted from the c.p. BaO_3 layers. Attach face-sharing pairs of octahedra, each sharing its lower vertices with vertices of three single octahedra. To the upper vertices of the pairs join another layer of single octahedra.

Determine the sequence of c.p. layers and hence the number of layers in the repeat unit, and compare with p. 68.

OCTAHEDRA SHARING FACES, EDGES, AND VERTICES

O.30. In the structure assigned to γ-$Cd(OH)_2$ each octahedral $Cd(OH)_6$ coordination group shares one face in addition to edges and vertices. The double chains formed from rutile chains sharing octahedron *faces* are linked in the same way as in rutile.

A portion of such a double chain, having the height of two octahedra in the direction perpendicular to the paper, is constructed from four octahedra using the types of connector indicated at the top-left corner of Fig. 76. Four chains are then linked through the 3-connectors to form the portion of structure shown to the right (heavier lines).

The corundum structure

O.31. The structure adopted by α-Al_2O_3 and some other sesquioxides provides an interesting example of octahedra sharing faces, edges, and vertices.

Construct a ring of six octahedra *ACACAC* using connectors as indicated in Fig. 77. Above the octahedra of type *A* and also above the hole *B* place

four more octahedra, each of the first three sharing one face with an octahedron of the first set. In the third layer place octahedra above the positions
C and B, using 4-connectors. In the resulting structure each X is common to
four octahedra. Each octahedron shares one face and three edges, and in

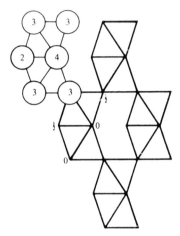

FIG. 76. The structure of γ-Cd(OH)$_2$.

addition each vertex is shared with one or two other octahedra. This model
should be compared with the model constructed from transparent spheres
in hexagonal closest packing (p. 63), the second (ii) of the three structures
in which two-thirds of the octahedral sites are occupied in a c.p. assembly. It
is instructive to make portions of the other two A$_2$X$_3$ structures.

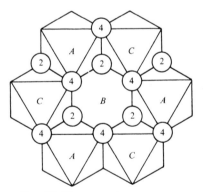

FIG. 77. The corundum structure.

In all three structures four octahedra meet at each vertex (X atom), and
since four edges meet at each vertex of an octahedron this implies that
sixteen edges meet at each X atom. However, in a c.p. structure there cannot

be more than twelve separate X–X edges meeting at each X atom, and therefore there must be sharing of edges or faces of the four octahedra meeting at each X atom in any c.p. A_2X_3 structure of this kind.

In this connection it is of interest to note that a simple *layer* structure A_2X_3 with 6-coordination of A and 4-coordination of X is not possible for purely topological reasons (see p. 167).

6. Miscellaneous Structures

STRUCTURES BUILT FROM TETRAHEDRA AND OCTAHEDRA

Tetrahedra and Octahedra sharing vertices only

M.1. IN THE two simple chains described below each tetrahedron shares two and each octahedron four vertices.

(a) Connect several octahedra to form part of an infinite chain in which each shares a pair of opposite vertices. Then join pairs of unshared vertices of adjacent octahedra to tetrahedra which lie alternately on opposite sides

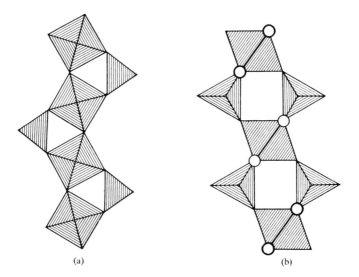

(a)   (b)

FIG. 78. Chains formed from tetrahedra and octahedra sharing only vertices.

of the chain, as in Fig. 78(a). Note that the vertices of an octahedron shared with tetrahedra are diametrically opposite ones.

What is the composition of the infinite chain? Give an example of a chain ion of this kind.

(b) Construct a portion of the chain of Fig. 78(b) in which successive octahedra are linked through pairs of tetrahedra. An octahedron is shown standing on an edge so that pairs of vertices are superposed in Fig. 78(b). The upper and lower vertices of these pairs are distinguished as heavy and light circles respectively to ensure that the correct combination of vertices of each octahedron is shared.

What is the composition of this chain? Give an example of an infinite chain ion of this kind which has been shown to exist in a crystalline salt.

M.2. A very simple 3D structure results if AX_4 tetrahedra share each vertex with an octahedral BX_6 group, the latter necessarily sharing its vertices with two other octahedra and four tetrahedra.

Construct a portion of this structure, given that each octahedron shares a pair of opposite vertices with other octahedra. Sketch the plan of the structure viewed along the direction of the octahedral chains.

What is the composition?

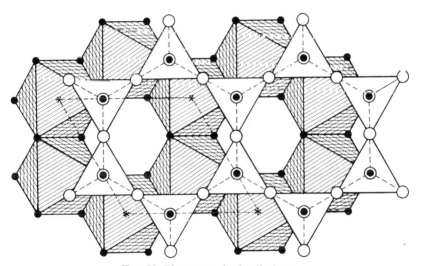

FIG. 79. The composite kaolin layer.

Tetrahedra sharing vertices, octahedra sharing edges
The kaolin and mica layers

M.3. Composite layers consisting of (largely) Mg or Al in octahedral and Si (or Al) in tetrahedral coordination are the structural units in numerous clay minerals, micas, and related compounds.

Construct the portion of octahedral layer shown in Fig. 79, using 3-connectors at all the (edge) junctions. This represents the arrangement of OH groups in $Al(OH)_3$ or, if further metal atoms are added at the centres of the 6-rings, in $Mg(OH)_2$. At the points marked $\odot$ attach tetrahedra, the remaining vertices of which are linked by 2-connectors to form a layer of tetrahedra having the atoms $\odot$ in common with the octahedral layer. Assuming all vertices of tetrahedra to be O atoms and the other vertices of the octahedra to be OH groups, determine the formula corresponding to the layer if there are Si atoms at the centres of the tetrahedra and (a) Al or (b) Mg atoms in the octahedra.

A similar layer of tetrahedra may be added to the other side of the octahedral layer. What is the composition of this triple layer?

*M.4. Construct three portions of rutile chain, each consisting of four octahedra, using 3-connectors, and add tetrahedra alternately to one side and the other (using 2-connectors) as in Fig. 80. Place the chains *a* and *c* on the table

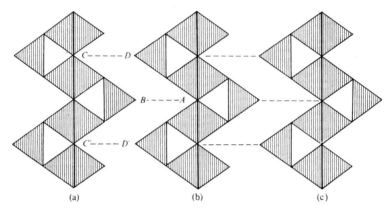

(a)   (b)   (c)

FIG. 80. Structure built from tetrahedra and octahedra.

and hold the central chain *b* at a higher level. Now join the remaining connector at the lower end of the shared edge *A* to the upper vertex of the vertical tetrahedron edge *B*. Make the similar connections between the upper connectors *C* and *C'* and the lower vertices *D* and *D'*, and the corresponding connections between the chains *b* and *c*. The chains are shown displaced laterally in Fig. 80; in the final model *A* is coincident with *B*, *C* with *D*, etc. The structure can continue indefinitely by adding further chains vertically above those shown in Fig. 80.

If there are A and B atoms at the centres of the octahedra and tetrahedra respectively and X atoms at all the vertices, what is the composition of the crystal?

Give an alternative description of the structure in terms of the packing of the X atoms, and the proportions of tetrahedral and octahedral holes occupied.

STRUCTURES BUILT FROM TRI-CAPPED TRIGONAL PRISMS

*M.5. We have noted earlier that this polyhedron (TCTP) represents the arrangement of ligands around the central metal atom in certain finite complexes. It is also the coordination group in a number of crystalline oxides and halides around metal ions which are too large for octahedral coordination but too small to form part of a c.p. assembly, in which they would be 12-coordinated. By sharing faces, edges, and/or vertices, the tri-capped trigonal prism forms extended groupings with X : A ratios having all values from 7 down to 2.

What is the composition of the chain formed when each TCTP shares the edges accentuated in Fig. 81?

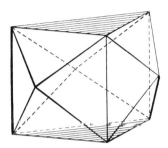

FIG. 81. The tri-capped trigonal prism.

What is the composition of the chain formed when the basal faces (shaded in Fig. 81) are shared?

Columns of this kind may be joined as shown in Fig. 82 by sharing vertices in much the same way as the chains of octahedra in the rutile structure.

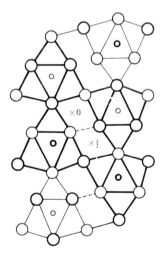

FIG. 82. A 3D structure built from columns of tri-capped trigonal prisms sharing vertices.

Construct a portion of this structure from four short lengths of chain, each containing two TCTPs. Note that two of the columns are displaced relative to the other two by an amount equal to one-half the height of the polyhedron.

Determine the composition of the structure, for example, by finding the number of kinds of non-equivalent X atom and the number of A atoms to which each is attached.

What is the arrangement of X atoms around points such as × at the height indicated, heights being measured in terms of the height c of one TCTP.

Compare this structure with that of $CaTi_2O_4$ constructed from octahedra (p. 103). How are the two related?

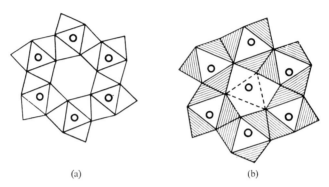

(a)   (b)

FIG. 83. 3D structures built from columns of tri-capped trigonal prisms sharing edges.

*M.6. If columns of (face-sharing) TCTPs are joined by edge-sharing as in Fig. 83(a) the structure of UCl_3 (and numerous $4f$ and $5f$ chlorides and some $4f$ trihydroxides) is formed. In principle the structure of $PbCl_2$ could be built from similar columns sharing edges with six instead of three others (Fig. 83(b)). However, when constructed from the rather symmetrical TCTPs provided the tunnels in the UCl_3 structure have regular hexagonal shape (as in the projection of Fig. 83(a)). In $PbCl_2$ the 9-fold coordination around the metal ions is distorted in such a way that by packing the columns of coordination polyhedra as in Fig. 83(b) the tunnels are of the same type as the columns themselves.

Part III: Additional Notes on Model-building

7. Polyhedra and Other Finite Systems

SYSTEMS OF CONNECTED POINTS

P.1. THE systematic approach is to consider the linking of the points to form in turn triangles, squares, pentagons, etc. This will lead to the following systems:

(a) tetrahedron, cube, pentagonal dodecahedron, and plane hexagonal net, which have angles of 60°, 90°, 108°, and 120° between links. The linear 3-connected systems of Fig. 4 (p. 12) are other possibilities for 4-gon and 5-gon circuits;

(b) octahedron and plane square net, with angles of 60° and 90° between links. The next simplest possibility, the diamond net (with all 6-gon circuits), is not likely to be constructed (angle between links, $109\frac{1}{2}°$).

(If polygonal circuits of more than one kind are allowed an indefinite number of polyhedra, 2D and 3D nets becomes possible.)

It is natural to inquire what happens if, for example, we try to build a plane net in which three 7-gons meet at every point. This point is discussed on p. 168.

P.2. The simplest solutions are the tetrahedron, octahedron, and icosahedron, and the plane 3-gon net. The attempt to build a net in which seven (or more) equilateral triangles meet at every point leads to curved surfaces (p. 175).

P.3. The first two solutions are the cube and plane square net. The cube may suggest a solution for five squares meeting at each point, the tubular system of Fig. 102 (p. 139), and for six squares meeting at each point, a stacking of cubes the edges of which correspond to the simple cubic lattice.

The solutions to these experiments should therefore include the five regular solids, the three regular plane nets, and possibly some of the more complex arrangements noted. The flexible connectors do not produce rigid models of 3-connected polyhedra, and the regular dodecahedron can conveniently be made from drilled balls and spokes using 'tetrahedral' holes, since $109\frac{1}{2}°$ is close to the internal angle of a regular pentagon (108°).

4-coordination

P.4. *Tetrahedron*

Fig. 84 shows a regular tetrahedron viewed (a) perpendicular to a face, and (b) along a line joining mid-points of opposite edges. The (maximum) distances between centres of tetrahedra sharing

	relative values
vertex: $l(\sqrt{3}/\sqrt{2})$,	1·00
edge: $l/\sqrt{2}$,	0·58
face: $l/\sqrt{6}$.	0·33

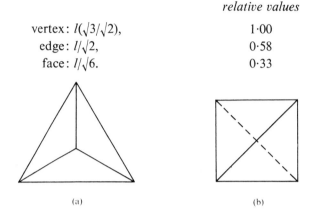

(a)   (b)

FIG. 84. Tetrahedron viewed in directions (a) perpendicular to face and (b) along a line joining mid-points of opposite edges.

6-coordination

P.6. *Octahedron and trigonal prism*

Fig. 85 shows an octahedron viewed along a line joining (a) opposite vertices, (b) mid-points of opposite edges, and (c) mid-points of opposite faces.

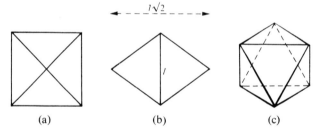

(a)   (b)   (c)

FIG. 85. Octahedron viewed along line joining (a) opposite vertices, (b) mid-points of opposite edges, and (c) mid-points of opposite faces.

The numbers of isomers are:
  (d) octahedron: 2 AX_4Y_2, 2 AX_3Y_3;
  (e) trigonal prism: 3 AX_4Y_2, 3 AX_3Y_3;
  (f) there are two geometrical isomers of an octahedral complex AX_2D_2, one of which is enantiomorphic.
    Distances between centres of octahedra sharing

	relative values
(g) vertex: $l\sqrt{2}$,	1·00
(h) edge: l,	0·71
(i) face: $l(\sqrt{2}/\sqrt{3})$.	0·58

8-coordination

P.8. *Cube and rhombohedron*

Fig. 86 shows a cube viewed along a body-diagonal. Since all the edges of a rhombohedron are of equal length, the polyhedron is completely specified by the edge length a and the angle α between a pair of (adjacent) edges. (For a cube $\alpha = 90$.)

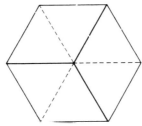

FIG. 86. Cube viewed along body-diagonal.

The additional vertices in Fig. 14(a) are those of an octahedron.

The polyhedron made with the four face-diagonals of the vertical faces in Fig. 14(b) and the diagonals AB and CD of the top and bottom faces would be a *hexagonal bipyramid*. This polyhedron cannot be constructed with eighteen equal edges because six equilateral triangular faces meeting at a vertex would be coplanar. The faces of a hexagonal bipyramid are isosceles, not equilateral, triangles.

The polyhedron represented by Fig. 14(c) is the square antiprism, one of the thirteen semi-regular Archimedean solids.

12-coordination

P.11. The icosahedron does not possess the 4-fold symmetry axes of the cube, but has axes of 2-, 3-, and 5-fold symmetry.

MOLECULAR SYMMETRY

P.14. Diagrams representing the operation of $\bar{1}$, $\bar{2}$, and $\bar{6}$ axes are shown in Fig. 8. To simplify drawing, points above and below the plane of the paper are indicated as filled and open circles, it being understood that there are no planes of symmetry perpendicular to the plane of the paper.

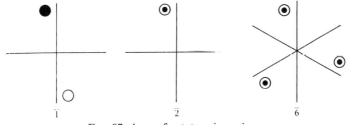

FIG. 87. Axes of rotatory inversion.

P.15. *Enantiomorphism*

There are four isomers of the tetramethyl-*spiro*-bipyrrolidinium cation, of which three are enantiomorphic. The fourth has a 4̄ symmetry axis (Fig. 88). If the mirror image of this isomer is made it will be found that it is identical with the original. This isomer is therefore inactive.

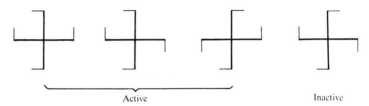

Active   Inactive

FIG. 88. Isomers of tetramethyl-*spiro*-bipyrrolidinium cation.

8. Repeating Patterns:
Two-dimensional
and Three-dimensional Nets

REPEAT UNITS AND FORMULAE

N.1. THE compositions of the repeating patterns of Fig. 19 are:

Chains: (c) A_2X_5, (d) AX_4, (e) AX_3,

Layers: (f) AX, (g) A_2X_3, (h) AX_2.

The octahedra are joined together by sharing

(d) a pair of opposite edges,

(e) a pair of opposite faces,

(h) six edges.

N.2. *Three-dimensional patterns*

The following data relate to the unit cells of the 3D structures of Fig. 20.

	Structure	Unit cell content	Nearest neighbours of A	Nearest neighbours of X
(a)	NaCl	4 AX	6 octahedral	6 octahedral
(b)	ReO_3	AX_3	6 octahedral	2 collinear
(c)	NbO	3 AX	4 coplanar	4 coplanar
(d)	Cu_2O	2 A_2X	2 collinear	4 tetrahedral

THE GEOMETRY OF THE 3-CONNECTED 6-GON LAYER

N.3. Fig. 89 shows elevations of the 3-connected 6-gon layer for the bond arrangements (a) p^0, (b) p^2, (c) p^1.

THREE-DIMENSIONAL NETS

The cubic 3-connected (10, 3) net

N.4. In the cubic (10, 3) net there are 4_1 axes in three directions and 3_1 axes in four directions—see the axial symmetry of the cube (p. 21).

Fig. 90 shows a projection of this net along a 3_1 axis. The cubic unit cell contains eight points. Each point is common to fifteen and each link to ten 10-gons.

The diamond net

N.5. For a projection of the structure of diamond see Fig. 29(b), p. 53. The structure is composed of chair-shaped rings of six atoms.

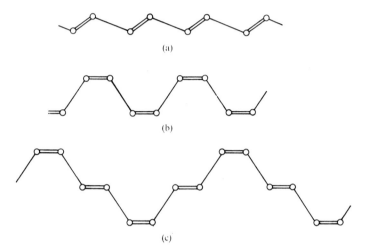

FIG. 89. Elevations of 6-gon layers.

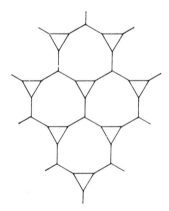

FIG. 90. Projection of cubic $(10, 3)$ net along 3_1 axis.

*N.6. *Formulae of borate ions*

	Finite hydroxy ion	*3D oxy-ion*
(a)	$B_3O_3(OH)_4^-$	$(B_3O_5)_n^{n-}$
(b)	$B_4O_5(OH)_4^{2-}$	$(B_4O_7)_n^{2n-}$
(c)	$B_5O_6(OH)_4^-$	$(B_5O_8)_n^{n-}$

A 3D anion formed from equal numbers of units (a) and (c) has the composition $(B_8O_{13})_n^{2n-}$.

The 3-connected net of Fig. 128(e), p. 172

N.8. This net is built of decagons. There are 8 points in the tetragonal unit cell of Fig. 128(e), i.e. $Z_c = 8$, compare $Z_t = 4$. There are two kinds of link in this net, one (type c) having $y = 8$ and the remainder $y = 6$. The weighted mean is $6\frac{2}{3}$ (p. 173).

FURTHER STUDY OF 4-CONNECTED 3D NETS WITH TETRAHEDRAL BOND ANGLES

Interpenetrating diamond nets

N.9. In the structure composed of two interpenetrating diamond nets the unit cell is the same as that of a single net if the differently coloured balls represent atoms of different elements. This cell is not body-centred but, like diamond, is cubic face-centred. If all the atoms are of the same kind, the unit

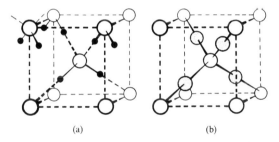

(a)   (b)

Fig. 91. Unit cells of the structures of (a) ice-VII and (b) Cu_2O.

cell reduces to one with edge equal to one-half that of the diamond net and therefore one-eighth the volume. It is body-centred only as regards the positions of the atoms, the arrangement of bonds from an atom at the origin being different from that of the bonds from the atom at the body-centre of the cell.

One of the high-pressure forms of ice (ice-VII) crystallizes with this 'pseudo-body-centred' structure, each H_2O molecule being hydrogen-bonded to only four of its eight equidistant neighbours. Since the O—H distance in the H_2O molecule is 1 Å and the length of a O $\cdots$ H—O bond is 2·9 Å the H atoms are not at the mid-points of the hydrogen bonds (Fig. 91(a)).

The unit cell of the structure consisting of two identical interpenetrating diamond nets with X atoms at the mid-points of the bonds (forming two collinear bonds to the A atoms) is shown in Fig. 91(b). The formula is AX_2. Compounds crystallizing with this structure include OCu_2 (cuprous oxide) and $Cd(CN)_2$.

N.10. The result of linking together atoms forming tetrahedral bonds and maintaining the *eclipsed* configuration at every pair of adjacent atoms is to form first a 5-gon ring. The angle of a regular pentagon is 108° so that very little distortion is involved if interbond angles of $109\frac{1}{2}°$ are used. The next stage is the formation of a pentagonal dodecahedron, followed by the formation of a set of dodecahedra surrounding the first one. However, a space-filling assembly of these polyhedra is not possible, because the dihedral angle is not an exact submultiple of 360°. Attempts to extend the model fail, for the result is not a periodic 3D structure but a radiating system of pentagonal dodecahedra, or alternatively a 4-connected network of pentagons, and this is not realizable with links of equal length.

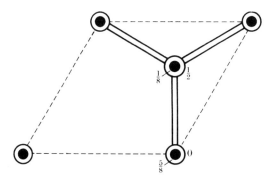

FIG. 92. Projection of one unit cell of the wurtzite structure.

Wurtzite structure

N.11. Join two atoms with bonds in the eclipsed position and keep the original bond *vertical*. Add the next six atoms, making the bond arrangement in each case *staggered*. The model can now be extended (horizontally) by adding six pairs of atoms. For each of these pairs the bonds are in the eclipsed position, and the model will obviously extend indefinitely in the horizontal plane. To extend the model in a vertical direction the simplest possibility is to make an eclipsed arrangement of bonds about each vertical bond, so that all vertical bonds are equivalent to the original one. This net represents the positions of the Si atoms in tridymite (SiO_2) and of the O atoms in ordinary ice (ice-I) or, if alternate atoms are Zn and S, of the hexagonal polymorph of ZnS (wurtzite). Fig. 92 shows the projection of a unit cell of the structure and the heights of the atoms. See also Fig. 5(c), p. 13.

Return now to the point at which the model reached the stage shown (in elevation) in Fig. 93(a), where a is the original vertical bond. The decision to treat the bonds b like the bonds a led to the wurtzite structure with a repeat distance in the vertical direction c_w (Fig. 93(b)). Alternatively we could have made a staggered bond arrangement at the ends of the bonds of type b instead of the eclipsed one (Fig. 93(c)), and this choice is available for each 'layer' of b bonds. There is accordingly an indefinite number of structures that may be regarded as hybrids between the diamond and wurtzite structures.

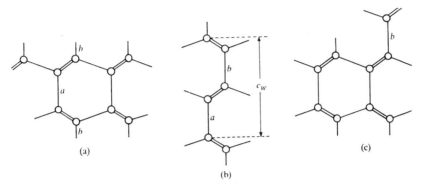

FIG. 93. Further study of 4-connected nets (see text).

Many structures of this type have been found in crystals of zinc sulphide and of carborundum (SiC). They are not normal polymorphs but arise from the mode of growth of the crystals, though there is not yet general agreement as to the type of stacking fault which can account for all the observed structures ('polytypes') and their relative abundances.

The Fedorov net

*N.13. In the structure built of tetrahedra the relative lengths of shared and unshared tetrahedron edges are $\sqrt{2} : \sqrt{3}$.

In the space-filling of (irregular) icosahedra and tetrahedra there are three times as many tetrahedra as icosahedra.

If an atom M occupies each of the truncated octahedral cavities and X atoms all points of the Fedorov net, the composition is MX_6. In $HPF_6.6H_2O$ the PF_6^- ions occupy the cavities and the H_2O molecules form the hydrogen-bonded framework. (The H^+ ions are presumably associated with the framework but they were not located in the X-ray study of the crystal structure.)

The 'pseudo-diamond' net

*N.14. The axial ratio $c : a = \sqrt{2}$.

The NbO net

N.15. (i) The NbO structure is related geometrically to the NaCl structure, from which it could be derived by removing one-quarter of the A and X atoms (see Fig. 5(b)).

(ii) The next nearest neighbours of a Nb atom are 8Nb at the vertices of a rectangular prism of height $\sqrt{2}$ times the edge of the base. The ratio of the Nb–Nb to the Nb–O distance is $\sqrt{2}$.

The adoption of this unique structure may be connected with the formation of Nb—Nb bonds (Nb—Nb = 2·98 Å, compare 2·85 Å in metallic Nb). Note the octahedral Nb_6 groups, which also occur in $Nb_{12}F_{15}$ and $Nb_6Cl_{14}.7H_2O$. (In NbO these Nb_6 groups are further linked into a 3D framework.)

The PtS structure

N.16. If difficulty is experienced in building this model reference may be made to Fig. 5(d), p. 13.

REPRESENTATION OF STRUCTURES BY PROJECTIONS

N.18. The structures shown in plan in Fig. 29 are (a) cubic 3-connected net, (b) diamond, (c) NbO, (d) simple cubic net, (e) body-centred cubic structure (or CsCl), and (f) cubic closest packing (face-centred cubic).

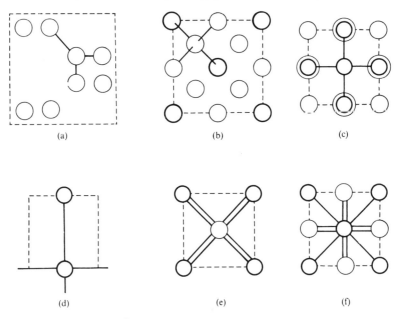

FIG. 94. Projections of unit cells of six cubic structures.

	(a)	(b)	(c)	(d)	(e)	(f)
(i) Coordination numbers	3	4	4	6	8	12
(ii) Number of atoms in unit cell	8	8	6	1	2	4

In Fig. 94 all the bonds are shown from one atom in each structure, except that in (d) there are also two bonds perpendicular to the plane of the paper.

9. Sphere Packings

THE CLOSEST PACKING OF EQUAL SPHERES

S.1. FIG. 95 shows a plan of the unit cell of h.c.p. It contains two atoms with the coordinates: 000, $\frac{1}{3}\frac{2}{3}\frac{1}{2}$.

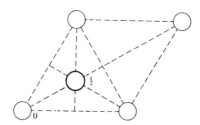

FIG. 95. Projection of unit cell of hexagonal closest packing.

Two alternative unit cells of c.c.p. are illustrated in Fig. 96(a) and (b). The cell contains four atoms.

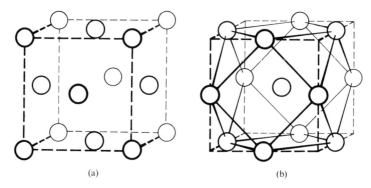

(a)   (b)

FIG. 96. Alternative unit cells of cubic closest packing.

In an infinite c.p. assembly the number of tetrahedral holes is equal to *twice* the number of c.p. spheres. The number of octahedral holes is equal to the number of c.p. spheres.

The radii of atoms which exactly fit into tetrahedral and octahedral holes are respectively 0·225 and 0·414 if the radius of the c.p. spheres is unity.

SOME FINITE GROUPS OF CLOSE-PACKED ATOMS

S.2. Fig. 97 shows layers of molecules (a) AX_6 and (b) A_2X_{10} arranged so that the X atoms are close-packed. Fig. 97(b) in fact represents a layer of Mo_2Cl_{10} molecules in the $MoCl_5$-graphite phase.

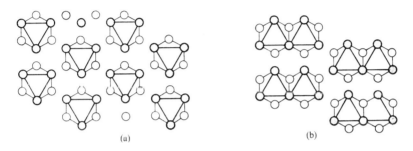

(a)   (b)

FIG. 97. Closest packing of (a) AX_6 and (b) A_2X_{10} molecules.

In 3D packings (molecular crystals) the fractions of holes occupied are: (i) $\frac{1}{8}$, (ii) $\frac{1}{6}$ of the tetrahedral holes, and (iii) $\frac{1}{6}$, (iv) $\frac{1}{5}$ of the octahedral holes. These fractions follow from the facts that the total numbers of T and O holes are respectively $2N$ and N for a close-packing of N spheres.

S.3. (a) In the A_3X_9 group each tetrahedral AX_4 group shares two vertices. Examples: the S_3O_9 molecule and the $Si_3O_9{}^{6-}$ ion (Fig. 101(b), p. 138).

(b) The formula is A_4X_{10}. The model represents the structure of the P_4O_{10} molecule, in which the oxygen atoms are c.c.p.

(c) The model represents a unit cell of c.c.p. (face-centred cubic) and is illustrated in Fig. 96(a).

(d) The unit cell (Fig. 96(b)) is related to that of Fig. 96(a) by a translation of one-half of the cell edge. Note that there is an atom at the body-centre of the cell but not at the origin. The structure is not body-centred but face-centred. The coordination polyhedron is a cuboctahedron.

(e) The centres of the twelve outermost spheres are the vertices of a truncated tetrahedron; there is also a sphere at the centre of each hexagonal face.

STRUCTURES A_mX_n IN WHICH X ATOMS ARE CLOSE-PACKED AND A ATOMS OCCUPY TETRAHEDRAL INTERSTICES

S.4. If all the tetrahedral holes in a h.c.p. assembly were occupied there would be sharing of faces between tetrahedral AX_4 groups. The sharing of faces between tetrahedral groups implies very short A—A distances and never occurs.

S.5. The AX_4 tetrahedra share only vertices, but three-quarters of the X atoms are bonded to three A atoms and the remainder to one A atom. This non-equivalence of X atoms is avoided in the HgI_2 structure, in which every I is bonded to two Hg atoms. The compounds AlOCl and GaOCl do, however, have a structure closely related to the (unknown) tetrahedral layer structure we have described but with one-half of the tetrahedra differently oriented from the remainder, as described on p. 141.

STRUCTURES A_mX_n IN WHICH X ATOMS ARE CLOSE-PACKED AND A ATOMS OCCUPY OCTAHEDRAL INTERSTICES

S.6. Table 11 summarizes the formulae of the structures formed when various proportions of the octahedral sites are occupied.

TABLE 11

Fraction of octahedral sites occupied	Between all successive layers		Between alternate pairs of layers only	
$\frac{1}{3}$	AX_3	⎧ 1D: ZrI_3 h.c.p. ⎨ 2D: — c.c.p. ⎩ 3D: RhF_3 h.c.p.	AX_6	Discrete molecules
$\frac{1}{2}$	AX_2	⎫	AX_4	Infinite chain molecule
$\frac{2}{3}$	A_2X_3	⎬ 3D structures	AX_3 ⎫	Layer
All	AX	⎭	AX_2 ⎭	structures

The AX_n complexes formed when the sites occupied between alternate pairs of layers are the small black circles of Fig. 34 and Fig. 35(a) are respectively: discrete AX_6 molecules, and infinite linear molecules AX_4 formed from octahedral groups sharing a pair of opposite edges.

In the $CrCl_3$ and $CdCl_2$ layers the octahedra share respectively three and six edges as shown by the heavy lines in Fig. 112(e) and (c).

One-third of the octahedral sites occupied

S.7. (ii) c.c.p. The structure consists of layers of octahedra (the layers being perpendicular to the c.p. layers) in which each octahedron shares two opposite edges and two opposite vertices (Fig. 98).

One-half of the octahedral sites occupied

S.8. The AX_2 structures arising from the four sequences are as follows.

1, 1'. This sequence implies h.c.p. In the resulting layer structure (layers perpendicular to the planes of c.p. atoms) columns of octahedra sharing a pair of opposite faces are further linked by sharing edges. There are two kinds

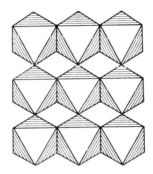

FIG. 98. Cubic close-packed layer structure AX_3.

of (non-equivalent) X atom, four vertices of each octahedron being common to four octahedra and the others to two octahedra: $(4 \times \frac{1}{4}) + (2 \times \frac{1}{2}) = 2$.

1, 2. This sequence also implies h.c.p. Chains of octahedra each sharing a pair of opposite edges are linked by vertex-sharing into a 3D structure in which each X is bonded to three A atoms. In this c.p. structure the three A atoms are nearly coplanar with the X atom. A slight rearrangement to make these neighbours exactly coplanar with X gives the rutile structure, which is adopted by a number of dihalides (largely difluorides, e.g. those of Mg, Fe, Co, Ni, Mn, and Zn) and dioxides (of Ti, Ge, Sn, and Pb).

Note that for regular octahedra the bond angles at the X atom are 90° and 135° (two). It is not possible to have the most symmetrical arrangement of A atoms around X (i.e. with three interbond angles of 120°) and at the same time regular octahedral coordination around A.

1, 3. The stacking of the layers corresponds to c.c.p. Octahedral AX_6 groups share four equatorial edges to form layers and the remaining vertices are shared to form a 3D structure. As in (1, 1') there are two kinds of non-equivalent X atom, four vertices of each octahedron being common to four and the remainder to two octahedra: $(4 \times \frac{1}{4}) + (2 \times \frac{1}{2}) = 2$.

1, 4. This sequence implies c.c.p. Every octahedron shares six edges, one with each of six adjacent octahedra, to form layers which are inclined to the plane of the c.p. layers used in the construction of the model. This is the $CdCl_2$ structure (see also p. 147) in which each X atom has three A neighbours all lying to one side. The numerous compounds crystallizing with this structure include dihalides (other than fluorides) and disulphides, e.g. the dichlorides of Mg, Fe, Co, and Ni, and the disulphides of Nb and Ta.

Two-thirds of the octahedral sites occupied

S.9. The structures are
  (i) a h.c.p. structure in which octahedra share a pair of opposite faces (in addition to the three edges shared with octahedra at the same level);
 (ii) a h.c.p. structure in which pairs of octahedra have one face in common; there is also vertex-sharing;
(iii) a c.c.p. structure in which there is further edge-sharing between octahedra.
In all three structures all X atoms have four A neighbours. In (i) there is a planar rectangular arrangement of the four A atoms all lying to one side of the X atom. In (ii) the arrangement is a (non-regular) tetrahedral one. In (iii) there are two types of non-equivalent X atom, one type having A neighbours at the corners of a square coplanar with the X atom, the other having a very unsymmetrical tetrahedral environment. The environment of X in (ii) approximates most closely to a regular tetrahedral one. As in the spinel and other structures the cation arrangement chosen appears to be that giving the most symmetrical distribution of *cations* around the *anion* as expected in an essentially ionic structure.

STRUCTURES $X_mY_nO_{3m}$ BUILT FROM CLOSE-PACKED XO_3 LAYERS

All octahedral O_6 holes occupied

S.12. In the c.c.p. structure *AcBaCb* each YO_6 octahedron shares a vertex with each of six other octahedra (perovskite structure). In the structure *AcBcAbCb* (*hc* sequence of c.p. layers) pairs of YO_6 octahedra sharing one face are further linked by vertex-sharing to six other pairs. This is the structure of the high-temperature form of $BaMnO_3$.

PERIODIC SPHERE PACKINGS WITH 8- AND 10-COORDINATION

S.15. In the 10-coordinated structure the distance to the (four) next nearest neighbours is 1·22, and $c:a$ is $\sqrt{2}/\sqrt{3}$. The packing in the plane $ABB'A'$ is shown in Fig. 99(a); the packing in the plane $ACC'A'$ is the same.

The crosses in Fig. 99(b) mark the positions of the centres of the spheres in the layer above (or below) the one shown.

Since there are three equivalent positions, *a, b,* and *c* (Fig. 99(b)), for the centres of spheres of layers adjacent to the one shown, there is an infinite number of layer sequences for these 10-coordinated assemblies. Three different sequences are found in $MoSi_2$, $CrSi_2$, and $TiSi_2$, the structure of the first of these compounds being the simple structure described above in which there is closest packing in two perpendicular planes.

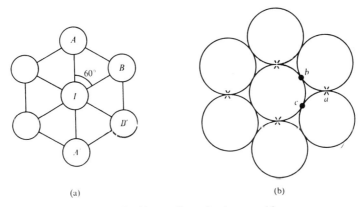

(a)   (b)

FIG. 99. The 10-coordinated sphere packing.

If c.p. layers are stacked so that spheres of successive layers fall directly above those of the layer below the packing is described as *simple hexagonal.* A sphere has eight nearest neighbours and twelve next nearest neighbours (at a distance 1·41).

In the MoS_2 structure a sulphur atom is in contact with ten other S atoms.

SOME NON-CRYSTALLOGRAPHIC SPHERE PACKINGS

*S.16. The total numbers of contacts in the assemblies of Fig. 43(a) and (b) are eleven and twelve respectively.

Data for the various sphere-packings are summarized in Tables 12 and 13.

TABLE 12

	Neighbours		
Structure	Number at 1·000	Next nearest	Density
Body-centred cubic	8	6 at 1·16	0·6801
$MoSi_2$	10	4 at 1·22	0·6981
Simple hexagonal	8	12 at 1·41	0·6046

TABLE 13. *Summary of stacking sequences of close-packed layers*

Positions of sphere centres in adjacent layers (see Fig. 100)	Number of nearest neighbours	Structure
1 1	8	Simple hexagonal
1 2†	10	MoSi$_2$, etc.
1 1, 3 3, etc.†	10	MoS$_2$, etc.
1 3†	12	Closest packing

† Infinite numbers of layer sequences.

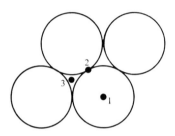

FIG. 100. Relative positions of sphere centres in adjacent close-packed layers (see Table 13).

10. Structures built from Tetrahedra

CONFIGURATIONS OF A_2X_7 IONS

T.1. (i) Angle A—X—A, 180°. Apart from planes of symmetry one form possesses a 3-fold and the other a $\bar{3}$ axis of symmetry.

(ii) Angle A—X—A less than 180°. Both the configurations of Fig. 46(a) and (b) have the symmetry mm; the angles A—X—A are 141° and $109\frac{1}{2}°$ respectively. The symmetry of configuration (c) is m, i.e. there is one plane of symmetry only.

INTERBOND ANGLES AT SHARED X ATOMS

*T.2. (i) If X atoms of tetrahedral AX_4 groups are shared between different groups the permissible values of the angle A—X—A are:

for face-sharing, 38°56′;
for edge-sharing, 65°58′–70°32′;
for vertex-sharing, 102°16′–180°.

The model required to calculate the lower limit of the angle A—X—A for edge-sharing is made by placing together two tetrahedra $ABCD$ and $BCDE$ sharing a face (BCD) and then placing one more tetrahedron in contact with the face ABC. Addition of a fourth tetrahedron on the face CDE gives the model required for the vertex-sharing calculation. (The angles 65°58′ and 102°16′ are respectively $\cos^{-1}\frac{11}{27}$ and $\cos^{-1}-\frac{17}{81}$.

(ii) For octahedra sharing X atoms the permissible values of the angle A—X—A are:

for face sharing, 70°32′;
for edge-sharing, 90°;
for vertex-sharing, 131°48′–180°.

The model required has octahedra in contact with the faces ABC and CDE of a pair of face-sharing tetrahedra. Note that the lowest angle A—X—A for vertex-sharing octahedra is 131° 48′ (*not* 135°). Compare with the values in the crystalline tri- and penta-fluorides of Ru, Rh, Ir, etc.

INFINITE PERIODIC STRUCTURES BUILT FROM TETRAHEDRA

Vertices common to two tetrahedra

T.3. *Two vertices shared*

Models constructed should include a portion of the infinite chain of Fig. 101(a) and a cyclic molecule or ion, e.g. S_3O_9, $Si_3O_9^{6-}$, $(PNCl_2)_3$, etc. (Fig. 101(b)).

T.4. *Three vertices shared*

The possibilities are now very numerous. Among the structures which are readily constructed are the following: from rings of 3 tetrahedra, the finite P_4O_{10} molecule (Fig. 2(b), p. 8); from rings of 4 tetrahedra, the infinite chain of Fig. 101(c) and the cubic A_8X_{20} molecule; from rings of 5 tetrahedra, the dodecahedral $A_{20}X_{50}$ molecule; from rings of 6 tetrahedra, the

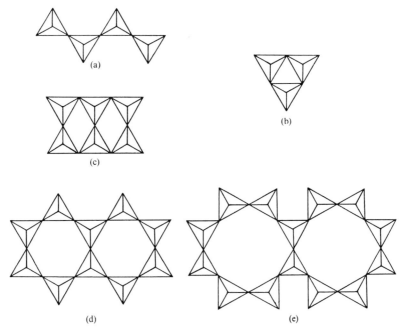

Fig. 101. Tetrahedra sharing two and/or three vertices.

hexagonal plane net; various layers based on 3-connected nets such as $\phi_4 = \phi_8 = \frac{1}{2}$. Models based on 3D nets, such as that of one form of P_2O_5 based on the 10-gon net of Fig. 4(e) present more difficulty. (Examples are not known of the A_8X_{20} or $A_{20}X_{50}$ molecules.)

'Hybrid' systems, in which some tetrahedra share two and others three vertices, include chains such as the $(Si_4O_{11})_n^{6n-}$ chain which is a characteristic feature of the structures of the amphiboles (Fig. 101(d)) and the $(Si_6O_{17})_n^{10n-}$ chain in the mineral xonotlite, $Ca_6Si_6O_{17}(OH)_2$ (Fig. 101(e)). This latter chain may be built from two simple chains cross-linked at every third tetrahedron.

T.5. *Four vertices shared*

A linear (tubular) system based on the 4-connected net of Fig. 102 may be constructed from tetrahedra each of which shares four vertices.

In the layer of Fig. 103(a) all the A—X—A bond angles are $109\frac{1}{2}°$. Examples, HgI_2 (red), γ-$ZnCl_2$. In the related layer of Fig. 103(b) the A—X—A bond angles are of two kinds, one half having the tetrahedral value while the others are 180°. This layer represents the arrangement of Zn

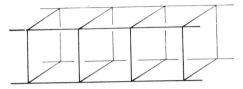

FIG. 102. A 4-connected linear system.

and O atoms in $SrZnO_2$. Its formation, in preference to the planar layer of Fig. 103(a), is presumably due to the need to provide suitable sites for the large Sr^{2+} ions between the layers.

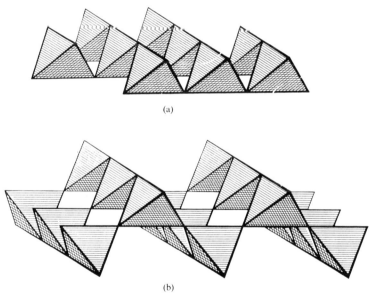

(a)

(b)

FIG. 103. Tetrahedral AX_2 layers: (a) HgI_2 (red), (b) $SrZnO_2$.

The *double layer* formed by joining together two hexagonal (3-connected) layers is the anion in one crystalline form of $CaAl_2Si_2O_8$.

T.7. *The cuprite and related structures*

*(ii) The composition of this structure is AB_2. This is the structure of the intermetallic compound $MgCu_2$. The larger (Mg) atoms are arranged at the points of the diamond net, and the Cu atoms are in one half of the positions

of cubic closest packing. There are closely related structures in which the A atoms delineate other 4-connected nets, e.g. the wurtzite net ($MgZn_2$).

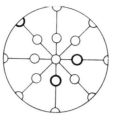

FIG. 104. Construction of truncated tetrahedron from drilled balls.

The coordination group around an A atom is a truncated tetrahedral group of twelve B atoms plus four A at a greater distance. The distance A—B = 2·345, A—A = 2·45, and the radius ratio $r_A : r_B = 1·345$. (A model of a truncated tetrahedron may be built from drilled balls using the holes (2-fold axes) indicated in Fig. 104. Note that edges common to two hexagonal faces correspond to face-diagonals of a cube.)

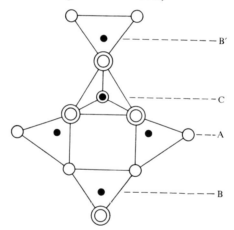

FIG. 105. Geometry of zeolite chain.

T.9. *Geometry of the zeolite chain*

It is convenient to take the length of the tetrahedron edge as two units. We calculate the distances of the projecting vertices A and C in terms of the repeat distance along the chain BB' (Fig. 105).

$$\frac{AB}{BB'} = \frac{2\sqrt{2}+\sqrt{3}}{6\sqrt{2}+2\sqrt{3}} = 0·38$$

and

$$\frac{BC}{BB'} = \frac{4\sqrt{2}+\sqrt{3}}{6\sqrt{2}+2\sqrt{3}} = 0·62,$$

these fractions having approximately the values $\frac{3}{8}$ and $\frac{5}{8}$.

Vertices common to three tetrahedra

T.10. The formulae of the layers are: (a) AX_2, (b) AXY. Number of contacts between unshared vertices: 2 (instead of 6).

There are only two possible arrangements of the three A atoms relative to an X atom (shared vertex), namely, all to one side of the plane of the shared vertices or one to one side and two to the other. The latter is the arrangement in the (puckered) layers of Fig. 106(a) and (b). Fig. 106(b) represents a layer in crystalline AlOCl or GaOCl.

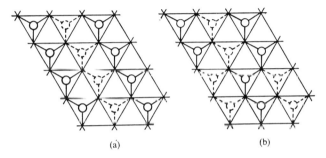

(a)   (b)

FIG. 106. Layers of tetrahedra sharing three vertices.

Tetrahedra sharing edges

T.11. The layer of Fig. 51, in which each tetrahedron shares four edges, has the composition AX. An X atom lies at the apex of a tetragonal pyramid having A atoms at the four corners of the base. Its bonds therefore all lie to one side of it, being directed along the slanting edges of the pyramid.

Examples: LiOH, OPb, OSn (the O atoms being at the centres of the tetrahedra in these two oxides).

In the 3D structure in which tetrahedra share all six edges:

(i) The A atoms are arranged at the vertices of a cube around X.

(ii) The X atoms are arranged in cubic closest packing.

(iii) This is the *antifluorite* structure (A_2X) of alkali oxides and sulphides such as Li_2O, Li_2S, etc. This model also represents the *fluorite* structure, but the formula is then preferably written F_2Ca to indicate that F^- is tetrahedrally coordinated and Ca^{2+} 8-coordinated.

T.12. Each X atom is bonded to four A atoms all lying to one side; the composition of the layer is therefore AX.

Tetrahedra sharing vertices and edges

*T.14. The composition of the layers of Fig. 55(b) or (c) is AX_2 and that of the 3D structures built from such layers by further vertex-sharing is A_2X_3.

TABLE 14. *Summary of tetrahedral structures*

Number of shared vertices	Type of complex	Formula	Examples
Vertices common to 2 tetrahedra			
1	Finite dimer	A_2X_7	Cl_2O_7, $Si_2O_7^{6-}$
2	Cyclic		S_3O_9, $(PNCl_2)_4$
	Infinite chain }	$(AX_3)_n$	$(SiO_3)_n^{2n-}$
3	Finite, infinite 1-, 2-, or 3D	$(A_2X_5)_n$	P_4O_{10} $Li_2(Si_2O_5)$ and P_2O_5 (layers) P_2O_5 (3D)
4	Infinite 1-, 2-, or 3D	$(AX_2)_n$	HgI_2 and $Sr(ZnO_2)$ (layers), SiO_2 (3D)
Vertices common to 3 tetrahedra			
3	Infinite 2D	$(AX_2)_n$	AlOCl, GaOCl
Edges common to 2 tetrahedra			
Number of shared edges			
1	Finite dimer	A_2X_6	Al_2Cl_6
2	Infinite chain	$(AX_2)_n$	$BeCl_2$, SiS_2
3	Double chain	$(A_2X_3)_n$	$Cs(Cu_2Cl_3)$
4	Layer	$(AX)_n$	LiOH, PbO
6	3D structure	$(A_2X)_n$	Li_2O, F_2Ca
Vertices and edges shared			
	3D structure	$(AX)_n$	β-BeO

11. Structures built from Octahedra

FINITE GROUPS OF OCTAHEDRA

O.1. The formulae of the groups illustrated in Fig. 56 are listed below together with examples which have been established by structural studies.

	Formula	Examples
(a)	A_2X_9	$Fe_2(CO)_9$, $(W_2Cl_9)^{3-}$, $(Tl_2Cl_9)^{3-}$
(b)	A_2X_{10}	Nb_2Cl_{10}, Mo_2Cl_{10}
(c)	A_2X_{11}	$(Nb_2F_{11})^-$
(d)	A_3X_{12}	$[Ni(acac)_2]_3$
(e)	A_0X_{13}	
(f)	A_3X_{14}	
(g)	A_3X_{15}	
(h)	A_4X_{16}	$[Ti(OC_2H_5)_4]_4$
(i)	A_4X_{16}	$[Co(acac)_2]_4$
(j)	A_4X_{17}	
(k)	A_4X_{18}	
(l)	A_4X_{22}	Mo_4F_{20}, $W_4O_4F_{16}$

($acac$ = acetylacetonate).

The structures of Fig. 56 in which all octahedra are topologically equivalent are: (a), (b), (c), (e), (g), (j), and (l).
O.2. Regarded as assemblies of octahedra the $Nb_6O_{19}^{8-}$ and $V_{10}O_{28}^{6-}$ ions are portions of the NaCl structure.

TABLE 8A. *Properties of the 12-octahedra complexes*

	(a)	(b)	(c)
Number of X atoms	38	40	40
Shape of central cavity	Octahedral	Tetrahedral	Tetrahedral
Type of packing of X atoms	c.c.p.	c.c.p.	†

† The central nucleus of sixteen X atoms is cubic close-packed but on the four close-packed faces of this truncated tetrahedral group the next layers (of six atoms) are placed in positions of h.c.p. (see p. 57).

*O.4. *The* PW$_{12}$O$_{40}$$^{3-}$ *ion*

(a) In the cuboctahedral complex corresponding to Fig. 60(a) the octahedra are arranged in the same way as in the NaCl structure. Fig. 107(a) shows a sketch of the complex viewed normal to a square face of the cuboctahedron.

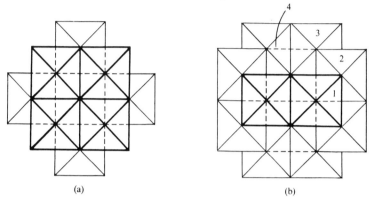

(a)   (b)

FIG. 107. Projections of the 12-octahedra complexes (a) and (b) of Table 8 and Fig. 60.

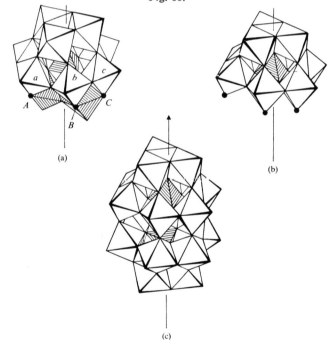

(a)

(b)

(c)

FIG. 108. The P$_2$W$_{18}$O$_{62}$$^{6-}$ ion.

(b) A projection of the complex is shown in Fig. 107(b).

*O.5. Fig. 108 shows the structure of the P$_2$W$_{18}$O$_{62}$$^{6-}$ ion.

OCTAHEDRA SHARING VERTICES ONLY

O.7. The structures are illustrated diagrammatically in Fig. 109 and listed in Table 15. Octahedra sharing a pair of adjacent vertices can form rings, (a), or a zig-zag chain, (b). The simplest ring is that formed of three octahedra; we illustrate the A_4X_{20} ring since examples of this ring are known. Sharing of two

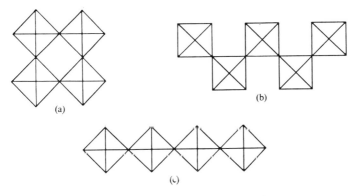

FIG. 109. Octahedra sharing two vertices.

opposite vertices gives an infinite chain of composition AX_5, (c), and if four equatorial vertices are shared the layer (d) is formed. If each octahedron shares a vertex with each of six neighbouring octahedra a 3D framework is formed. There is a number of such structures, of which the simplest is the ReO_3 structure. In this structure the centres of the octahedra (Re atoms) lie at the points of the simplest 6-connected 3D net, the most symmetrical form of which is the (primitive) cubic lattice.

TABLE 15. *Structures formed from octahedra sharing vertices only*

Number shared	Structure	Figure	Examples
2 (*cis*)	A_4X_{20} ring	109(a)	Mo_4F_{20}
	AX_5 chain	109(b)	CrF_5, VF_5, $MoOF_4$
2 (*trans*)	AX_5 chain	109(c)	BiF_5, $\alpha\text{-}UF_5$
4 (equatorial)	AX_4 layer	—	SnF_4, NbF_4, $UO_2(OH)_2$, $K_2(NiF_4)$
6	AX_3 framework	62	ReO_3, WO_3, $Sc(OH)_3$

If four equatorial vertices of each octahedron are shared the A atoms are arranged on a 4-connected plane net, which in the examples of Table 15 is the simplest (4-gon) net of that type. Layer structures based on more complex nets are not known, but just as the ReO_3 structure can be assembled from

SnF_4 layers so 3D structures can be built from these more complex 4-connected octahedral layers, by joining the octahedra through the two unshared vertices. These 3D structures are found in tungsten bronzes and in compounds such as $NaNb_6O_{15}F$. Fig. 72 (p. 105) shows the projection of a unit cell of the ReO_3 structure and of part of the hexagonal bronze structure adopted by $K_{0.3}WO_3$ and the similar rubidium and caesium compounds.

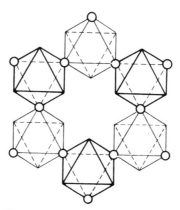

FIG. 110. Octahedral A_2X_9 layer.

O.8. In the ReO_3 structure the oxygen atoms occupy three-quarters of the positions of cubic closest packing. If the remaining sites are occupied (at the centres of the cubic unit cells) the *perovskite* structure for compounds such as $RbCaF_3$ is formed. This structure, or a slightly distorted variant, is adopted by numerous complex fluorides and oxides, for example, $BaTiO_3$, $KNbO_3$, and $CaTiO_3$, the mineral after which the structure is named.

The modified form of the ReO_3 structure shown in Fig. 62(b) is more suitable for hydroxides because hydrogen bonds can be formed across the shorter diagonals of the rhombuses (broken lines).

*O.9. The layer structure in which each octahedron shares three vertices with three other octahedra is illustrated in Fig. 110. Its formula is A_2X_9. Sharing of the remaining vertices leads to the ReO_3 structure.

OCTAHEDRA SHARING EDGES ONLY

O.11. *Two edges shared*

(i) Note that there are two ways of selecting two edges with a common vertex. If the angle between the edges is 60° a trimeric group A_3X_{13} is formed in which there are three kinds of non-equivalent X atom, as already mentioned on p. 93. If the angle between the edges is 90° the tetramer A_4X_{17} is formed, also with three types of non-equivalent X atom, or the infinite chain of Fig. 111(c) with only two kinds of non-equivalent X atom and composition AX_4. The A_3X_{13} and A_4X_{17} complexes are illustrated in Fig. 111(a) and (b).

(ii) The sharing of two opposite edges gives the infinite chain of composition AX_4, which represents the structure of the macromolecule in crystalline NbI_4 and of the infinite anion in $K_2(HgCl_4).H_2O$. The numerals in Fig. 112(a) indicate the numbers of A atoms to which an X atom is bonded.

For another way of selecting two edges which have no common vertex, see p. 98.

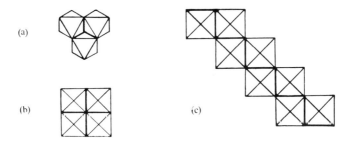

FIG. 111. Octahedra sharing two edges with a common vertex: (a) A_3X_{13}, (b) A_4X_{17}, (c) $(AX_4)_n$ chain.

O.12. *Three edges shared*

The unique selection of edges is that of Fig. 112(e). The sharing of these edges by every octahedron gives the planar AX_3 layer of which crystalline $AlCl_3$, $Al(OH)_3$, etc. are constructed.

The mid-points of these edges are coplanar with the central A atom. Octahedra sharing these three edges can therefore form 3D structures based on any 3-connected net that can be constructed with equal bonds and inter-bond angles of 120°, for example, the cubic (10, 3) net of Fig. 4(d). No examples are known of 3D structures of this kind.

O.13. *Six edges shared*

The two sets of six edges are those of Fig. 113(a) and (b). Sharing of the edges (a) gives the AX_2 layer of which the CdI_2 and $CdCl_2$ structures are built. It is illustrated in Fig. 112(c), which also shows the arrangement of bonds formed by an X atom.

O.14. *Four edges shared*

(i) The double chain of composition AX_3 is illustrated in Fig. 112(b) together with its end-on view. Examples include the infinite anion in $NH_4(CdCl_3)$ and the cation in $[Mg_2(OH)_3(H_2O)_3]Cl.H_2O$. There are three kinds of non-equivalent X atom which belong to one, two, or three octahedra as indicated at the right of Fig. 112(b).

(ii) The sharing of these four edges gives the layer of Fig. 112(d), which may conveniently be built from O_3 units. By counting the number of X atoms associated with each group of three A atoms, allowing for the sharing of some of them between two or three A_3X_n groups, the composition is found to be A_3X_8 $(4+6(\frac{1}{2})+3(\frac{1}{3})$ X atoms for every 3 A atoms). This layer represents the structure of crystalline Nb_3Cl_8.

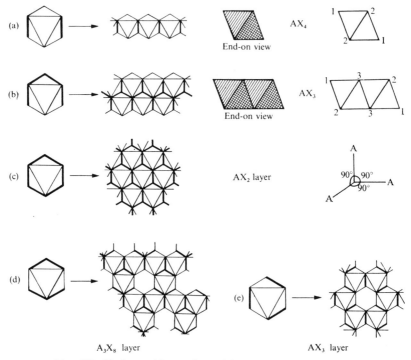

FIG. 112. Chains and layers formed by octahedra sharing edges.

In the layers of Fig. 112(c), (d), and (e) the X atoms are close-packed. The layers may therefore be described in terms of the fractions (all, $\frac{3}{4}$, or $\frac{2}{3}$) of the octahedral holes occupied between alternate pairs of layers of c.p. X atoms.

(iii) Four edges meeting at one vertex are shared by each octahedron in the finite group of six octahedra illustrated in Fig. 57(a). The composition is A_6X_{19} (see also *O.2). Note the three different X : A ratios (3, $2\frac{2}{3}$, and $3\frac{1}{6}$) in (i), (ii), and (iii), in all of which each octahedron shares four edges.

Further examples of structures in which octahedra share only edges

*O.15. Two edges shared

The chains formed by adjacent octahedra sharing the edges *fab*, *fac*, *fad*, and *fae* of Fig. 64 are illustrated in Fig. 114. The angle of inclination of the 3_1 screw axis of the chain *fad* to its projection in the plane of the paper is $\tan^{-1} 1/\sqrt{2} = 35°16'$.

O.16. *Six edges shared*

The composition of the corrugated layer of Fig. 65 may be determined by noting that four X atoms of each octahedron are shared between four octahedra while two are shared between two octahedra: $(4 \times \frac{1}{4}) + (2 \times \frac{1}{2}) = 2$, whence the composition is AX_2.

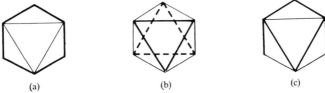

(a)   (b)   (c)

FIG. 113. Three ways of selecting six edges of an octahedron.

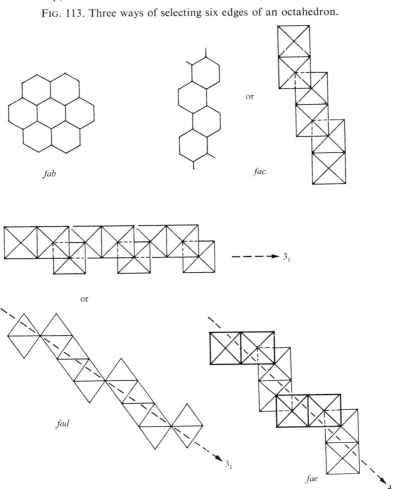

FIG. 114. Further structures in which octahedra share two edges.

The atacamite and spinel structures

*O.17. *The atacamite structure*

(i) The composition is AX_2.

(ii) The X atoms are arranged in cubic closest packing, and between successive pairs of c.p. layers alternately three-quarters and one-quarter of the octahedral holes are occupied by A atoms.

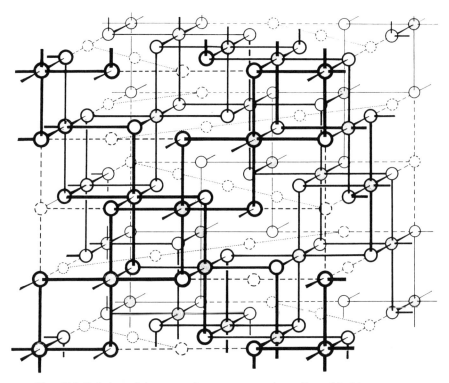

FIG. 115. Relation of the atacamite structure to the sodium chloride structure.

(iii) The structure can be derived from the NaCl structure by removing one-half of the A atoms (ions) in rows as indicated in Fig. 115.

(iv) The structure is a diamond-like arrangement of octahedral AX_6 groups meeting to form tetrahedral cavities at the points of that net. It can therefore be built by placing AX_6 octahedra with their A atoms at the mid-points of the links of the diamond net and sharing the six edges of two opposite faces with six other octahedra.

(v) An X atom is bonded to three A atoms all lying to one side, the inter-bond angles in the ideal structure being 90°. This arrangement of nearest neighbours is the same as in the $CdCl_2$ structure.

*O.18. *The spinel structure*

The composition is A_2BX_4. In the ideal structure the interbond angles A—X—A are three of 90° and three of 125°16′.

OCTAHEDRA SHARING VERTICES AND EDGES

The rutile structure

O.19. In the most symmetrical form of this structure built with regular octahedra an X atom has three coplanar A neighbours, interbond angles being one of 90° and two of 135°.

The unit cell of the rutile structure contains $2AX_2$.

(i) The axial ratio $c : a = \sqrt{2}/(1+\sqrt{2}) = 0.58$ for the structure with regular octahedra (Fig. 116).

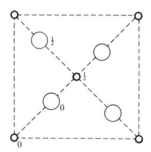

FIG. 116. Projection of the rutile structure.

(ii) The coordinates of the atoms are:

A   000, $\frac{1}{2}\frac{1}{2}\frac{1}{2}$

X $\pm (xx0, \frac{1}{2}+x, \frac{1}{2}-x, \frac{1}{2})$. $x = 1 - \frac{1}{4}\sqrt{2} = 0.293$.

(iii) For an equilateral triangular arrangement of Ti around 0 $c : a = \sqrt{(2/3)} = 0.817$, and $x = \frac{1}{3}$. (For any form of the rutile structure having tetragonal symmetry the coordinates of X are as in (ii) and there is the following relation between the x coordinate of X and the axial ratio: $8x = 2 + (c/a)^2$.)

Framework structures built from 'double rutile' chains

*O.20. In the idealized structure of CaV_2O_4 (Fig. 68(b)) the oxygen atoms are arranged around Ca at the vertices of a tri-capped trigonal prism. In the actual structure Ca has eight oxygen neighbours at distances from 2·39 to 2·64 Å and a ninth at 3·21 Å.

*O.21. In the $CaTi_2O_4$ structure of Fig. 69(b):

(a) there are three types of non-equivalent O atoms, bonded to 2, 3, and 4Ti atoms; $\frac{1}{2}+(3\times\frac{1}{3})+(2\times\frac{1}{4}) = 2$;

(b) the arrangements of Ti atoms around each type of O atom are shown in Fig. 117;

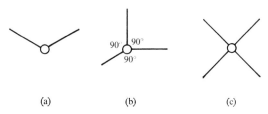

(a)   (b)   (c)

FIG. 117. Nearest neighbours of O atoms in $CaTi_2O_4$.

(c) the O atoms are arranged around Ca at the vertices of a tri-capped trigonal prism (but see also p. 155).

*O.22. The compositions of the layers of Fig. 70 are: (a) AX_2—$(\frac{2}{2}+\frac{4}{4} = 2)$, (b) AX_2—$(1+\frac{5}{5} = 2)$, (c) AX_3, (d) A_3X_8, and (e) A_2X_5. The layer (b) is a portion of the NaCl structure. Oxy-hydroxides of vanadium provide examples of some of these layers: (c) $VO(OH)_2$, (d) $V_3O_4(OH)_4$, and (e) $V_2O_2(OH)_3$; compare the diaspore structure of $VO(OH)$.

Structures built from 'double ReO_3' chains

O.23. Projections of the other two structures analogous to that of Fig. 73(a) are shown in Fig. 118.

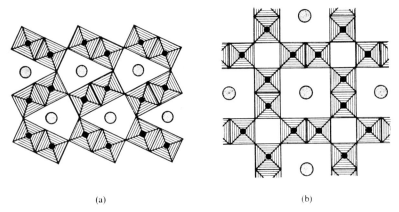

(a)   (b)

FIG. 118. Framework structures built from double ReO_3 chains.

O.24. The *framework* of Fig. 73(a) has the composition AX_3. In the structure of $CaTa_2O_6$ built from regular octahedra Ca is surrounded by 9O at the vertices of a tri-capped trigonal prism. In the actual structure (Fig. 74) Ca has eight approximately equidistant neighbours (at 2·4–2·6 Å) and a ninth at a distance of 3·3 Å.

O.25. The composition of the layer of Fig. 73(b) is AX_3. The only compound known to crystallize with this layer structure is MoO_3.

The 3D structure of Fig. 73(c) has the composition A_2X_5. This is the idealized structure of V_2O_5; in the actual structure the octahedra of oxygen atoms around vanadium atoms are much less regular.

More complex structures

*O.26. The composition of the infinite chain of Fig. 75(a) is AX_3. The composition of the 3D framework of Fig. 75(b) is AX_2. (In each octahedron four vertices are common to four octahedra and two vertices are common to two octahedra: $(4(\frac{1}{4}) + 2(\frac{1}{2}) = 2)$.)

This model represents the crystal structure of $CoMoO_4$, the sequence of A atoms along a chain being

$$\text{Mo} \quad \text{Co} \quad \text{Co} \quad \text{Mo} \quad \text{Mo} \quad \ldots$$
$$\text{Mo} \quad \text{Mo} \quad \text{Co} \quad \text{Co} \quad \text{Mo} \quad \ldots$$

This structure could be derived from the NaCl structure. From a horizontal layer remove $\frac{5}{9}$ of the A atoms and $\frac{1}{9}$ of the X atoms, giving A_4X_8 from $9AX$.

*O.27. The composition of the layer may be derived in the following way. Of A_6X_{22}, the composition of the 6-octahedron sub-unit, 8X are shared with other similar units, giving A_6X_{18} or AX_3. This layer represents the structure of the anion in the red molybdenum bronze, $K_{0.26}MoO_3$.

*O.28. The 3D framework corresponding to the plan of Fig. 75(c), in which each octahedron shares one edge and four vertices, has the composition AX_3. It represents the idealized structure of the anion in the cubic polymorph of $KSbO_3$, which also crystallizes with the ilmenite and pyrochlore structures. The potassium ions are accommodated in the large tunnels parallel to the body-diagonals of the cubic unit cell.

Topologically this structure is related to the NbO net. A unit consisting of two edge-sharing octahedra can join to four similar units by sharing vertices as shown in Fig. 75(c).

12. Miscellaneous Structures

STRUCTURES BUILT FROM TETRAHEDRA AND OCTAHEDRA

Tetrahedra and octahedra sharing vertices only

M.1. (a) THE composition may be deduced in the following way.

There are equal numbers of tetrahedra and octahedra. Each tetrahedron has two shared vertices and each octahedron four shared vertices; the composition must therefore be $A_2(3X + 4X)$ or A_2X_7. The model represents the structure of the anion in $Na_2Mo_2O_7$.

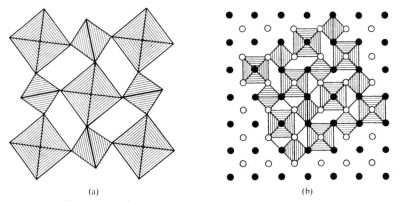

(a)   (b)

FIG. 119. Projection of the crystal structure of $VOMoO_4$.

(b) The composition of the chain is A_3X_{10}. The model represents the structure of the anion in $K_2Mo_3O_{10}$.

In this crystalline salt the Mo in 'tetrahedral' coordination has oxygen neighbours at the distances 1·64, 1·70, 1·90, and 1·95 Å and also a fifth at 2·08 Å. If the latter is counted as part of the coordination group these five oxygen atoms are arranged at the vertices of a very distorted trigonal bipyramid.

M.2. The 3D structure has the composition ABX_5. It is illustrated in Fig. 119(a) as found for crystalline $VOMoO_4$. Related compounds with essentially the same structure include $MoOPO_4$, $NbOPO_4$, and $VOSO_4$. In crystals of all these compounds there is considerable distortion of the transition-metal–oxygen octahedra.

Alternatively the structure may be described as a slightly distorted cubic closest packing of O atoms in which $\frac{1}{10}$ of the tetrahedral holes are occupied by Mo (P, S) atoms and $\frac{1}{5}$ of the octahedral holes by V (Mo, Nb) atoms (Fig. 119(b)).

Tetrahedra sharing vertices, octahedra sharing edges

The kaolin and mica layers

M.3. The formula corresponding to the composite layer of Fig. 79 may be determined by noting that the unit cell of the octahedral layer (asterisks at corners) contains 2Al (or 3Mg) and 6OH. In the composite layer two of the 6OH have become O atoms of SiO_4 tetrahedra, so that we have $Al_2(OH)_4O_2$ (or $Mg_3(OH)_4O_2$). For each of these O atoms there is 1Si and $\frac{3}{2}O$ in the tetrahedral layer, whence the formula of the double layer is $Al_2(OH)_4(SiO_{2.5})_2$, i.e. $Al_2(OH)_4Si_2O_5$ (or $Mg_3(OH)_4Si_2O_5$).

If tetrahedra are added on both sides of the octahedral layer the formula of the triple layer is $Al_2(OH)_2(SiO_{2.5})_4$, i.e. $Al_2(OH)_2Si_4O_{10}$ (or $Mg_3(OH)_2Si_4O_{10}$).

*M.4. The composition of the crystal is ABX_4. Since the model is made from chains consisting of equal numbers of octahedra and tetrahedra there must be equal numbers of A and B atoms. Each X atom belongs to one tetrahedron only, and therefore the formula must be ABX_4. The structure is alternatively described as an assembly of A atoms (ions) and BX_4 tetrahedra, and is the structure of many oxy-salts, e.g. $MgSO_4$, $MnSO_4$, $CrPO_4$, and $ZnCrO_4$.

The structure is approximately a c.c.p. assembly of X atoms in which B atoms occupy $\frac{1}{8}$ of the tetrahedral holes and A atoms $\frac{1}{4}$ of the octahedral holes.

STRUCTURES BUILT FROM TRI-CAPPED TRIGONAL PRISMS

*M.5. The compositions of the chains are: two edges of Fig. 81 shared, AX_7, as in K_2PaF_7; two faces shared, AX_6, as in $[Sr(H_2O)_6]Cl_2$.

The composition of the 3D framework of Fig. 82 is AX_4. Of the nine vertices of each TCTP six are common to two and three to three polyhedra, whence $6(\frac{1}{2}) + 3(\frac{1}{3}) = 4$.

The arrangement of X atoms around the points $\times$ is octahedral.

This is the same structure as that of $CaTi_2O_4$ constructed from octahedra on p. 103. Here we have built it as an assembly of CaO_9 coordination polyhedra of composition $(CaO_4)_n$, as compared with a framework of octahedral TiO_6 groups of composition $(Ti^{III}O_2)_n$. It should be noted that in the actual crystal structure the environment of Ca^{2+} is less symmetrical than the TCTP we have used here, the coordination being in fact 8- rather than 9-coordination. The distances from Ca^{2+} to its eight nearest neighbours are 2·32 Å. (2), 2·46 Å. (4), and 2·74 Å. (2), with the ninth neighbour at 3·15 Å.

Appendix 1

POLYHEDRA

THE mathematician recognizes various classes of polyhedra, but we are concerned here only with the simple convex bodies with which we are all familiar. The numbers of vertices (N_0), edges (N_1), and faces (N_2) of a convex polyhedron satisfy Euler's relation:

$$N_0 + N_2 = N_1 + 2.$$

This may be proved in a variety of ways, of which the following is an example.

A polyhedron may be represented by a diagram of the type shown in Fig. 120 (Schlegel diagram), where the perimeter R represents one face and all the other faces are shown as lying within it. (We may imagine the polyhedron resting on the face R and viewed with exaggerated perspective.) This particular polyhedron has one r-gon face and all the other faces are triangular; there are P_r vertices in the perimeter and P_i in the interior of the Schlegel diagram. The sum of the interior angles of the face R is $180°(P_r - 2)$. Around each inner point the sum of the angles is $360°$, and therefore the sum of all the angles within R is equal to $180°(P_r + 2P_i - 2)$. Since the sum of the interior angles of a triangle is equal to $180°$ it follows that the number of triangles is $P_r + 2P_i - 2$. The number of faces (N_2) on the polyhedron is $P_r + 2P_i - 1$, since the outer polygon is one face. The total number of edges (N_1) may be counted in the following way. Each triangle with one side in the perimeter contributes one plus two halves, and each triangle in the interior, three halves, whence

$$N_1 = 2P_r + \tfrac{3}{2}(2P_i - 2) = 2P_r + 3P_i - 3.$$

The number of vertices $N_0 = P_r + P_i$ and therefore

$$N_0 + N_2 = 2P_r + 3P_i - 1 = N_1 + 2.$$

Other polyhedra with the same number of vertices may be derived from the one represented by Fig. 120 by removing edges such as AB, when both N_2 and N_1 decrease by one. Removal of edges involving 3-connected vertices, followed by removal of the resulting 2-connected vertices, gives other polyhedra with fewer vertices, and it may be verified that all such operations are consistent with Euler's equation.

Relations between the numbers of faces of different kinds on polyhedra may be found in the following way. Consider the general case, a polyhedron having f_n n-gon faces and v_p vertices at which p edges meet. Since every edge is common to two faces and joins two vertices, the number of edges may be counted in two ways:

$$N_1 = \Sigma \tfrac{1}{2} p v_p = \Sigma \tfrac{1}{2} n f_n$$

and we may write

$$N_1 = \frac{2}{m} \left(\Sigma \tfrac{1}{2} n f_n \right) + \left(1 - \frac{2}{m} \right) \Sigma \tfrac{1}{2} p v_p,$$

where $2/m$ is any fraction.

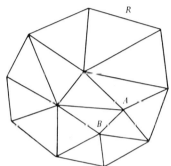

FIG. 120. Schlegel diagram of polyhedron.

Substituting in Euler's formula we have

$$N_2 - \left\{ \frac{2}{m} \left(\Sigma \tfrac{1}{2} n f_n \right) + \left(1 - \frac{2}{m} \right) \Sigma \tfrac{1}{2} p v_p \right\} + N_0 = 2,$$

and remembering that $N_2 = \Sigma f_n$ and $N_0 = \Sigma v_p$,

$$\Sigma (m - n) f_n + \Sigma \{ m - (\tfrac{1}{2} m - 1) p \} v_p = 2m.$$

For $m = 6$ this becomes

$$\Sigma (6 - n) f_n + \Sigma (6 - 2p) v_p = 12,$$

the expanded form of which is

$$3f_3 + 2f_4 + f_5 = 12 + 0v_3 + 2v_4 + 4v_5 + \ldots \pm 0f_6 + f_7 + 2f_8 + \ldots .$$

If all the vertices are 3-connected

$$3f_3 + 2f_4 + f_5 \pm 0f_6 - f_7 - 2f_8 - \ldots = 12. \tag{1}$$

Substitution for $m = 4$ and $m = 3\tfrac{1}{3}$ instead of 6 in the earlier equation gives the corresponding equations for 4- and 5-connected polyhedra:

$$\text{4-connected:}\quad 2f_3 \pm 0f_4 - 2f_5 - 4f_6 - \ldots = 16, \tag{2}$$

$$\text{5-connected:}\quad f_3 - 2f_4 - 5f_5 - 8f_6 - \ldots = 20. \tag{3}$$

Equations (1)–(3) are all of the general form

$$\Sigma f_n\{4-(2-n)(2-p)\} = 4p.$$

In the analogous equation for 6-connected polyhedra the coefficient of f_3 is zero and all the other coefficients have negative values. There is therefore no simple convex polyhedron having six (or more) edges meeting at *every* vertex.

The special solutions of equations (1)–(3), namely,

$$3\text{-connected}: f_3 = 4; f_4 = 6; f_5 = 12,$$

$$4\text{-connected}: f_3 = 8,$$

$$5\text{-connected}: f_3 = 20,$$

correspond to polyhedra having all vertices of the same kind and all faces of the same kind. In their most regular forms (regular polygonal faces) these are the five regular (Platonic) solids: tetrahedron, cube, (pentagonal) dodecahedron, octahedron, and icosahedron. The figures in Table 16 show that there is a special (reciprocal) relationship between certain pairs of these solids, the number of edges being the same but one of the pair having f faces and v vertices and the other v faces and f vertices. The cube is reciprocal to the octahedron, the dodecahedron to the icosahedron; the tetrahedron is clearly reciprocal to itself.

TABLE 16. *The regular (Platonic) solids*

	n, p	N_0	N_1	N_2	Dihedral angle	Vertex	For edge length 2 distance† from centre to Mid-point of edge	Mid-point of face
Tetrahedron	3, 3	4	6	4	70°32′	$3^{\frac12}/2^{\frac12}$	$1/2^{\frac12}$	$1/6^{\frac12}$
Octahedron	3, 4	6 ⎫ 12		8	109°28′	$2^{\frac12}$	1	$2^{\frac12}/3^{\frac12}$
Cube	4, 3	8 ⎭		6	90°	$3^{\frac12}$	$2^{\frac12}$	1
Icosahedron	3, 5	12 ⎫ 30		20	138°12′	$5^{\frac14}\tau^{\frac12}$ (1·902)	τ (1·618)	$\tau^2/3^{\frac12}$ (1·511)
Dodecahedron	5, 3	20 ⎭		12	116°34′	$3^{\frac12}\tau$ (2·802)	τ^2 (2·618)	$\tau^{\frac52}/5^{\frac14}$ (2·226)

† The number τ is the positive root of the equation $\tau^2-\tau-1 = 0$ and is equal to $2\cos\pi/5$ or $(1+\sqrt{5})/2$. It has an interesting connection with the dimensions of polygons and polyhedra with 5-fold symmetry. It is the distance between alternate vertices of a regular pentagon of unit side and is the distance from centre to vertex of a regular decagon of unit side. Because of this connection with the pentagon it enters into the formulae for the surface areas and volumes of regular dodecahedra and icosahedra and also the dimensions of these polyhedra. The ratios of alternate pairs of successive numbers in the Fibonacci series

$$1, 1, 2, 3, 5, 8, 13, 21, 34, \ldots$$

rapidly approach the value τ (1·61803).

The regular solids have all vertices equivalent (isogonal) and all faces of the same kind (isohedral). If we retain the first condition but allow regular polygonal faces of more than one kind we find a set of semi-regular polyhedra, the Archimedean solids (Table 17). The symbols show the types of faces

TABLE 17. *The Archimedean semi-regular solids*

	Symbol	Name	Faces	Number of vertices	Edges
1	3.6^2	Truncated tetrahedron	8	12	18
2	3.8^2	Truncated cube	14	24	36
3	4.6^2	Truncated octahedron	14	24	36
4	$(3.4)^2$	Cuboctahedron	14	12	24
5	$4.6.8$	Truncated cuboctahedron	26	48	72
6	3.4^3	Rhombicuboctahedron	26	24	48
7	$3^4.4$	Snub cube	38	24	60
8	3.10^2	Truncated dodecahedron	32	60	90
9	$(3.5)^2$	Icosidodecahedron	32	30	60
10	5.6^2	Truncated icosahedron	32	60	90
11	$4.6.10$	Truncated icosidodecahedron	62	120	180
12	$3.4.5.4$	Rhombicosidodecahedron	62	60	120
13	$3^4.5$	Snub dodecahedron	92	60	150
14	—	Regular prisms	$m+2$	$2m$	$3m$
15	—	Regular antiprisms	$2m+2$	$2m$	$4m$

meeting at each vertex, the index being the number of faces. These solids comprise a group of thirteen polyhedra derivable from the regular solids by symmetrically shaving off their vertices (a process called 'truncation'), of which only the first five are of importance in crystals, and the families of prisms and antiprisms. These last two groups have, in their most regular forms, a pair of parallel regular m-gon faces at top and bottom and are completed by m square faces (regular prisms) or $2m$ equilateral triangular faces (regular antiprisms). The second prism, in its most symmetrical form, is the cube, and the first antiprism is the octahedron. (For completeness we may add that there is a second arrangement of the faces of one of the Archimedean solids, giving the so-called pseudo-rhombicuboctahedron.) The regular solids and some of the Archimedean solids are illustrated in Fig. 121.

The fact that the number of isogonal bodies is limited to the five regular solids and the Archimedean solids is of considerable importance in chemistry. There are many molecules and complex ions in which five atoms or groups surround a central atom. The fact that it is not possible to distribute five equivalent points uniformly over the surface of a sphere, apart from the trivial case when they form a regular pentagon, is obviously relevant to a discussion of the configuration of such finite groups or more generally of any structure in which atoms have five nearest neighbours. Similar considerations apply to 7-, 9-, 10-, and 11-coordination.

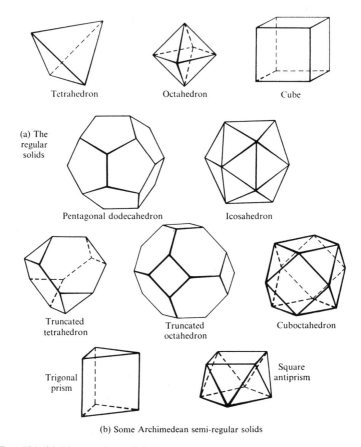

Tetrahedron   Octahedron   Cube

(a) The regular solids

Pentagonal dodecahedron   Icosahedron

Truncated tetrahedron   Truncated octahedron   Cuboctahedron

Trigonal prism   Square antiprism

(b) Some Archimedean semi-regular solids

FIG. 121. (a) The regular solids; (b) some Archimedean semi-regular solids.

Corresponding to the semi-regular polyhedra of Table 17 there are sets of reciprocal bodies named after Catalan, who first described them all in 1865. Of these we need note only the rhombic dodecahedron, which is the reciprocal of the cuboctahedron, and the family of bipyramids which are related in a similar way to the prisms.

One other family of polyhedra is of special interest in structural chemistry. In equation (1) for 3-connected polyhedra the coefficient of f_6 is zero. The truncated tetrahedron has the same value of f_3 (namely, 4) as the tetrahedron but also has four 6-gon faces. The truncated octahedron has $f_4 = 6$ and $f_6 = 8$

(compare the cube, $f_4 = 6$), and the truncated icosahedron has $f_5 = 12$ and $f_6 = 20$ (compare the dodecahedron, $f_5 = 12$). The zero coefficient of f_6 suggests that there might be, for example, a family of polyhedra having $f_5 = 12$ and various numbers of 6-gon faces. However, although all these polyhedra would be consistent with equation (1) they cannot necessarily be constructed, and in fact the first member of the family, $f_5 = 12$, $f_6 = 1$, is not realizable. The next three members of the family are of interest in connection with the structures of certain clathrate hydrates. Certain combinations of these polyhedra with dodecahedra form space-filling arrangements in which four edges meet at each vertex. These 3D frameworks can be formed by water molecules, each forming four hydrogen bonds, situated at the vertices of the polyhedra. These structures may be described as expanded ice-like frameworks containing polyhedral cavities which accommodate molecules such as Cl_2, Br_2, or $CHCl_3$.

The reciprocals of these 3-connected polyhedra are triangulated polyhedra with twelve 5-connected and two, three, four, etc., 6-connected vertices. Together with icosahedra ($v_5 = 12$) they are found as coordination polyhedra in numerous transition metal alloys.

Appendix 2

PLANE NETS

WE HAVE shown that the number of triangles in Fig. 120 is $P_r + 2P_i - 2$. Now suppose that the number P_i of interior points is made very large compared with the number P_r of points in the perimeter, so that P_r/P_i tends to zero. The number of triangles becomes $2P_i$, since $P_r - 2$ may be neglected, i.e. any indefinitely extended system of points (N in number) can be connected up to form a system of $2N$ triangles. (There is apparently no corresponding rule for a three-dimensional array of points. For example, if N points are joined together to form aN tetrahedra there is no unique value of a.)

Since each triangle has three edges and each edge is common to two triangles, the number of edges in the assembly of triangles is $3N$:

$$\left. \begin{array}{l} N \text{ points,} \\ 3N \text{ edges,} \\ 2N \text{ triangles.} \end{array} \right\} \tag{A}$$

We now wish to find the corresponding numbers for any assembly of polygons *of all kinds* in which *three* edges meet at every point. Since each edge joins two points and three edges meet at each point there must be $3N/2$ edges in a system of N points. The problem is to determine the total number of polygons.

If we remove one edge from the assembly of polygons the number of polygons falls by one. Therefore, to change from the assembly of triangles (A) with $3N$ edges to our assembly of polygons with $3N/2$ edges we have to remove $3N/2$ edges, and in so doing we remove the same number of polygons. Hence the number of polygons must be $N/2$, since there were $2N$ polygons (triangles) in (A). We have therefore:

$$\left. \begin{array}{l} N \text{ points,} \\ 3N/2 \text{ edges} \\ N/2 \text{ polygons,} \end{array} \right\} \text{ for a 3-connected array of polygons.}$$

For 4-, 5-, and 6-connected systems there must be respectively $2N$, $5N/2$, and $3N$ edges, and comparing with (A) we find:

N points	N points	N points
$2N$ edges	$5N/2$ edges	$3N$ edges
N polygons	$3N/2$ polygons	$2N$ polygons

for 4-connected, 5-connected, and 6-connected nets.

We may now derive a general equation for 3-connected plane nets. Let ϕ_n be the fraction of the total number of polygons which are n-gons, and therefore $\phi_n(N/2)$ the actual number of n-gons. If we add together terms

$$3\phi_3(N/2) + 4\phi_4(N/2) + \ldots n\phi_n(N/2),$$

each edge is counted twice (since each is common to two polygons), therefore

$$(3\phi_3 + 4\phi_4 + 5\phi_5 + \ldots n\phi_n)\, N/2 = 2(3N/2)$$

or

$$\Sigma n\phi_n = 6.$$

For 4-, 5-, and 6-connected nets the corresponding values of $\Sigma n\phi_n$ are found in the same way to be 4, 10/3, and 3.

It is convenient to have these equations written out in full:

3-connected: $3\phi_3 + 4\phi_4 + 5\phi_5 + 6\phi_6 + 7\phi_7 + 8\phi_8 + 9\phi_9 + \ldots n\phi_n = 6,$ (4)

4-connected: $= 4,$ (5)

5-connected: $= 10/3,$ (6)

6-connected: $= 3.$ (7)

There are three, and only three, special solutions of these equations corresponding to plane nets in which all the polygons have the same number of edges (and the same number of lines meet at every point), namely:

$$\text{3-connected:}\ \phi_6 = 1,$$
$$\text{4-connected:}\ \phi_4 = 1,$$
$$\text{6-connected:}\ \phi_3 = 1.$$

They are illustrated in Fig. 122(a). The last is the only plane 6-connected net, and evidently the equations of the type we have derived do not permit plane nets with more than six lines meeting at every point. We return to this point shortly.

For 3-, 4-, and 5-connected nets there are other solutions of the equations corresponding to combinations of polygons of two or more kinds. For example, the next simplest solutions for 3-connected nets are: $\phi_5 = \phi_7 = \frac{1}{2}$, $\phi_4 = \phi_8 = \frac{1}{2}$, and $\phi_3 = \phi_9 = \frac{1}{2}$. The first of these, $\phi_5 = \phi_7 = \frac{1}{2}$, is discussed in the next section. The most symmetrical configuration of the second is illustrated with the other semi-regular nets in Fig. 122(b), and the third is shown in Fig. 90 as the projection of the cubic (10, 3) net along the direction of the 3_1 axes. Of the indefinitely large number of plane nets a limited number can be drawn with regular polygons. Analogous to the five regular and thirteen semi-regular (Archimedean) polyhedra there are three regular plane nets (the special solutions listed above) and eight semi-regular nets in which there are regular polygons of two or more kinds (Fig. 122(b)).

The reciprocal relations between plane nets are also reminiscent of those between polyhedra. Using the symbol (n, p) for a regular net (or polyhedron) in which p n-gons meet at each point, we see that the nets $(6, 3)$ and $(3, 6)$ are related in this way while the reciprocal of $(4, 4)$ is the same net (compare the

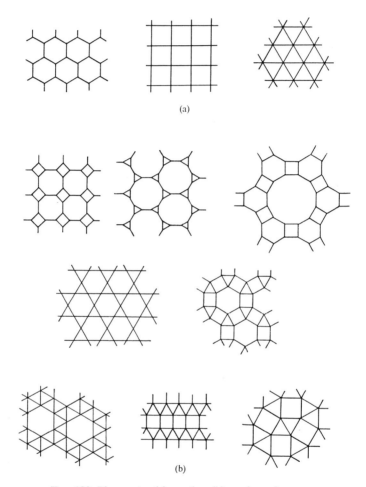

FIG. 122. Plane nets: (a) regular, (b) semi-regular.

tetrahedron). The reciprocals of the eight semi-regular nets of Fig. 122(b), formed by drawing the perpendicular bisectors of the links in these nets, represent divisions of the plane into congruent polygons—compare the relation of the Catalan to the Archimedean solids.

It will be observed that the semi-regular nets (Fig. 122(b)) include two configurations of a 5-connected net consisting of 3-gons and 4-gons (bottom right-hand corner). Their reciprocals are plane nets consisting entirely of pentagons (congruent but not regular) which complete the series:

p	n-gons
3	6
3, 4	5
4	4
6	3

In order to derive the general equation for nets containing both 3- and 4-connected points we must allow for variation in the proportions of the two kinds of points. If the ratio of 3- to 4-connected points is q it is readily shown that in a system of N points the number of links is $N(3q+4)/2(q+1)$. Proceeding as before it is found that $\sum n\phi_n = 2(3q+4)/(q+2)$. The value of $\sum n\phi_n$ ranges from 6, when $q = \infty$, to 4, when $q = 0$, and has the special value 5 if the ratio of 3- to 4-connected points is 2 : 1. The special solution of the equation $\sum n\phi_n = 5$ is $\phi_5 = 1$, corresponding to the nets mentioned above.

Although (3, 4)-connected plane nets are not of much interest in structural chemistry the 3D nets of this type form the basis of a number of crystal structures.

Configurations of plane nets

The equations (4)–(6) are concerned only with the proportions of polygons of different kinds and not at all with the arrangement of the polygons relative to one another. The reader may reasonably ask why we have illustrated nets as *repeating* patterns. For the special solutions of equations (4)–(6) there is no question of different arrangements of the polygons since each net is composed of polygons of one kind only. However, the *shape* of the hexagons in $\phi_6 = 1$ determines whether the net is a repeating pattern and if it is, the size of the repeat unit. Fig. 123 shows portions of periodic forms of this net; clearly a net in which the hexagons are distorted in a random way has no periodicity, or alternatively it has an infinitely large repeat unit (unit cell).

The situation is more complex if the net contains polygons of more than one kind. All the semi-regular nets except one (see Fig. 122) have a unique configuration (arrangement of polygons) but this is due to the insistence on regular polygons. If we drop this requirement and consider, for example, the net $\phi_4 = \phi_8 = \frac{1}{2}$ simply as a system of 4-gons and 8-gons we find that there is an indefinitely large number of ways of arranging equal numbers of the two kinds of polygon, and the same is true of nets such as $\phi_5 = \phi_7 = \frac{1}{2}$, $\phi_3 = \phi_9 = \frac{1}{2}$, and so on. Four of the simplest ways of arranging equal numbers of 5-gons and 7-gons are shown in Fig. 124. (Two of these, (a) and (d), are closely related, being built of the same sub-units, the strip A and its mirror-image B.) As in the case of the net $\phi_6 = 1$ the value of Z (the number of points in the repeat unit) is also dependent on the *geometry* of the polygons. Thus the

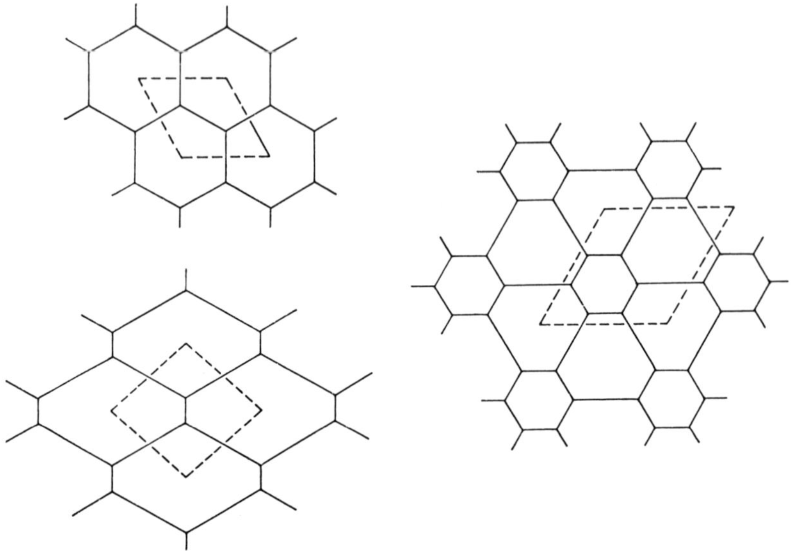

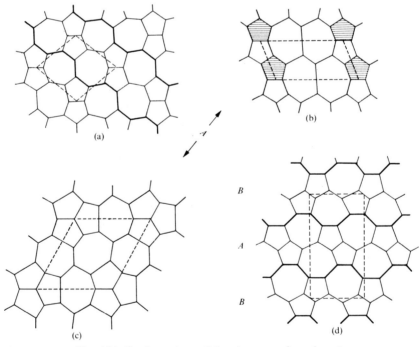

FIG. 123. Forms of the plane 6-gon net.

(a)

(b)

(c)

(d)

A

B

A

B

FIG. 124. Configurations of the plane net: $\phi_5 = \phi_7 = \frac{1}{2}$.

net illustrated in Fig. 124(b) has $Z = 8$ only if all the shaded pentagons are both congruent and similarly oriented. The reader may easily confirm that if alternate 4-gons in the net $\phi_4 = \phi_8 = \frac{1}{2}$ are squares of two different sizes the content of the unit cell is doubled, to $Z = 8$. When illustrating a particular configuration of a net we choose the most symmetrical form having the smallest unit cell.

Plane nets composed of alternate points of two kinds

As noted in the introduction, the non-existence of simple layer structures for compounds A_2X_3 in which the coordination numbers of A and X are 6 and 4 has a topological rather than a crystal chemical explanation. We may define a simple layer structure as one in which all the atoms can be projected

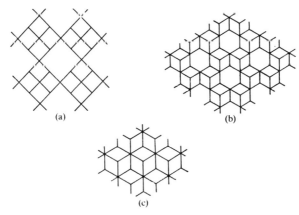

(a)   (b)

(c)

FIG. 125. The three plane nets with alternate p- and q-connected points.

into a plane without any links intersecting. The atoms of a layer A_xX_y are then represented as forming a 2D tessellation in which the points are of two kinds and all links represent A—X bonds. Fig. 125(c) then corresponds to the layer of CdI_2 (or $CdCl_2$). We now demonstrate that there are only three nets of this kind in which the coordination numbers of both types of atom are 3 or more, and that these do not include a (6, 4)-connected net.

If p- and q-connected points alternate in a plane net all the polygons must have even numbers of sides, and therefore the maximum attainable ratio of links : points is reached when the number of edges of each polygon is the smallest possible, namely, 4. We first show that for any plane net composed of 4-gons the ratio of links to points is 2 regardless of the connectedness of the points.

In the reciprocal net all points are 4-connected and their number is that of the original 4-gons (say, N). The number of links in the reciprocal net is equal to the number of links in the original net. This number is $2N$ since every 4-gon has four edges and each edge is common to two 4-gons. We require to find the number of polygons (N^*) in the reciprocal net, which is equal to the number of *points* in the original net. The number of points (N) in the reciprocal net is equal to $N^*\Sigma n\phi_n/4$ where ϕ_n is the fraction of n-gons. But for a 4-connected net $\Sigma n\phi_n = 4$, whence $N^* = N$. The number of polygons in the reciprocal net and therefore of points in the original net is accordingly N, and the ratio of links : points is equal to 2.

For a periodic net consisting of alternate p- and q-connected points the fractions of these points are $q/(p+q)$ and $p/(p+q)$ respectively, and therefore the number of links is $pqN/(p+q)$, whence the ratio of links : points is $pq/(p+q)$. The only combinations of (different values of) p and q ($\geqslant 3$) giving $pq/(p+q) \leqslant 2$ are: 3 and 4, 3 and 5, and 3 and 6. The corresponding nets are illustrated in Fig. 125:

(a) $v_3 = \frac{4}{7}, v_4 = \frac{3}{7}; f_4 = \frac{4}{5}, f_8 = \frac{1}{5}; \quad Z = 7;$

(b) $v_3 = \frac{5}{8}, v_5 = \frac{3}{8}; f_4 = \frac{6}{7}, f_6 = \frac{1}{7}; \quad Z = 8;$

(c) $v_3 = \frac{2}{3}, v_6 = \frac{1}{3}, f_4 = 1; \quad\quad\quad Z = 3.$

Radiating plane nets

In the derivation of equations (4)–(6) we supposed that P_r/P_i tends to zero as P_i increases. We now consider the possibility that this ratio does not tend to zero, and we may do this by constructing planar arrangements in which, for example, p triangles meet at each point. Instead of considering an enclosed area divided into triangles we shall start from a central point, making all the polygons triangles and ensuring that each point is p-connected. If $p = 3$ the system obviously terminates at the stage shown in Fig. 126(a), which is simply the Schlegel diagram of a tetrahedron. For $p = 4$ the points shown as open circles must all be connected to a single point, conveniently placed below the plane of the paper, and similarly for $p = 5$. The diagrams (b) and (c) represent an octahedron and icosahedron respectively. For higher values of p the counting of P_r and P_i is made easier if the points are placed on series of concentric circles. For $p = 6$ the pattern continues indefinitely and evidently Fig. 126(d) is the periodic (3, 6) net. From the numbers of points on successive circles, 6, 12, 18, 24, etc., it can easily be checked that P_r/P_i tends to zero. However, for $p \geqslant 7$ we find a quite different state of affairs. The numbers of points on successive circles increase rapidly (for example, 7, 21, 56, 147, etc. for $p = 7$, Fig. 126(e)), and these numbers are multiples of alternate terms in the Fibonacci series: 1, 1, 2, 3, 5, 8, 13, 21, 34, 55, ... Successive values of P_r/P_i tend to the value τ.†

† See footnote to Table 16, p. 158.

Systems $(3, p)$ having $p \geqslant 7$ are therefore not consistent with our assumption that P_r/P_i tends to zero, and the same is true of, for example, the reciprocal 3-connected nets if the polygons have more than six edges and for 4-connected nets $(n, 4)$ if $n > 4$. It should be mentioned here that tessellations such as

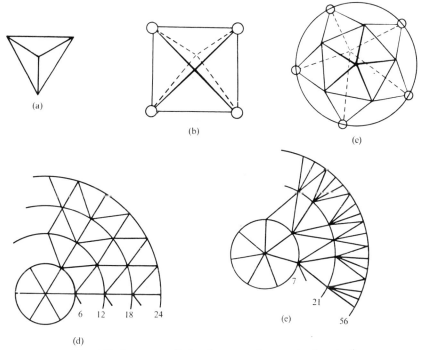

FIG. 126. Systems radiating from a unique centre (see text).

$(3, p)$, where $p > 6$, and others which are not realizable as solutions of equations (4)–(6) can be realized on surfaces of other kinds. The relevant hyperbolic surfaces are not of interest here since they cannot be constructed in ordinary space, but there are some interesting surfaces based on 3D nets and described later on which, for example, all the tessellations from $(3, 7)$ to $(3, 12)$ can be inscribed.

In the introduction we remarked on the possible relevance of radiating systems, more particularly three-dimensional ones, to the structures of phases such as glasses or crystalline polymers. There is a brief mention of some 3D radiating systems in Appendix 3.

Appendix 3

THREE-DIMENSIONAL NETS

No equations are known analogous to those for polyhedra and plane nets relating to the proportions of polygons (circuits) of different kinds. A different approach is therefore necessary if we wish to derive the basic three-dimensional nets.

Any pattern that repeats regularly in one, two, or three dimensions consists of units that join together when repeated *in the same orientation*, i.e. all units are identical and related only by translations. In order to form a 1-, 2-, or 3-dimensional pattern the unit must be capable of linking to 2, 4, or 6 others, because a 1-dimensional pattern must repeat in both directions along a line, a 2-dimensional pattern along 2 non-parallel lines, and a 3-dimensional pattern along 3 (non-coplanar) lines (axes). The repeat unit may be a single point or a group of connected points, and it must have at least 2, 4, or 6 free links available for attachment to its neighbours. (The requirement of a minimum of 4 free links for a 2D pattern may at first sight appear incompatible with the existence of 3-connected plane nets, but we have seen (Fig. 123) that even in the simplest of these nets ($\phi_6 = 1$) the *repeat unit* consists of a pair of connected points, this unit having the minimum number (4) of free links.)

Evidently the simplest unit that can form a 3D pattern is a single point forming 6 links, but for 4- and 3-connected 3D nets the units must contain respectively 2 and 4 points, as shown in Fig. 127. The series is obviously completed by the intermediate unit consisting of one 4- and two 3-connected points, which also has the necessary minimum number (6) of free links. These values of Z, the number of points in the repeat unit, enable us to understand the nature of the simplest 3D nets. Similarly oriented units must be joined together through the free links, each one to six others. This implies that the 6 free links from each unit must form 3 pairs, one of each pair pointing in the opposite direction to the other. Identically oriented links repeat at intervals of $(Z+1)$ points, so that circuits of $2(Z+1)$ points are formed. We therefore expect to find the family of basic 3D nets listed in Table 18.

We noted in the introduction (p. 7) that the number of points (atoms) in the crystallographic unit cell may be larger than the number in the topological unit cell, and that there may be alternative cells with different contents, which we may distinguish as Z_c. The values of Z_t in Table 18 refer to the smallest (topological) repeat unit; the values of Z_c are those for the cells of Fig. 128.

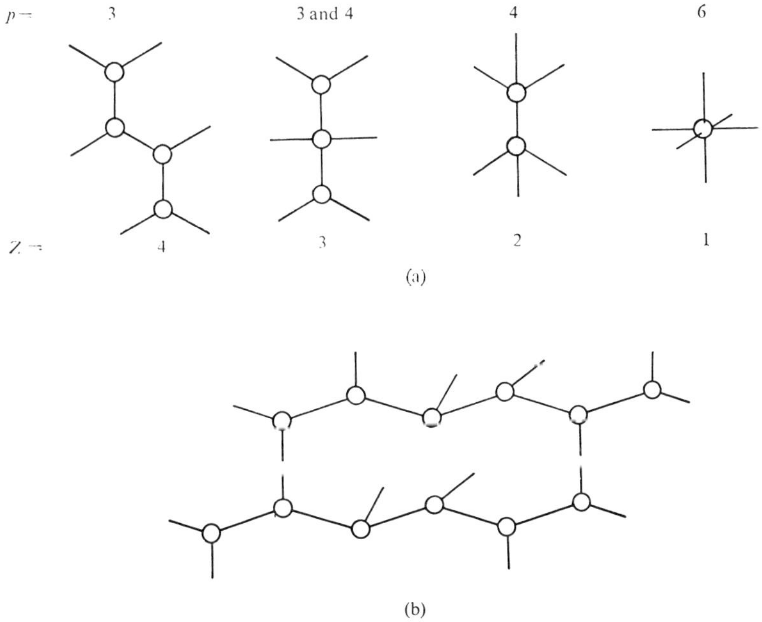

(a)

(b)

FIG. 127. Structural units for 3-dimensional nets (see text).

TABLE 18. *The basic 3-dimensional nets*

p	n	Z_t	Z_c	y	x	Fig. 128
3	10	4	8	10	15	(a)
3, 4	8	3	6	8	$13\frac{1}{3}$†	(b)
4	6	2	8	6	12	(c)
6	4	1	1	4	12	(d)

† Weighted mean.

By analogy with the regular polyhedra and plane nets we might expect to find a set of regular 3D nets which have all their links equal in length, all circuits (defined as the shortest paths including 2 non-collinear links from any point) identical, and the most symmetrical arrangement of links around every point. Three of the nets of Table 18 satisfy all these criteria, namely, the 3-connected net (10, 3), the diamond net (6, 4), and the simple cubic framework or primitive cubic lattice (4, 6); all have cubic symmetry. They are illustrated in Fig. 128(a), (c), and (d). There is a second net (10, 3), the ThSi₂

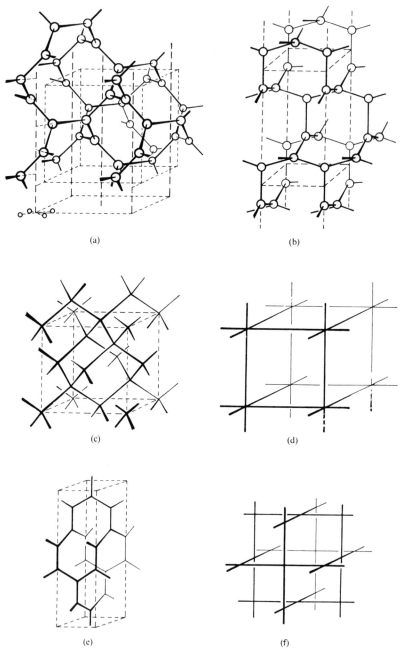

(a)

(b)

(c)

(d)

(e)

(f)

FIG. 128. Three-dimensional nets: (a)–(d), the four nets of Table 18, (e) ThSi$_2$ net, and (f) NbO net.

net (Fig. 128(e)), which in its most symmetrical form has equal coplanar bonds and bond angles of 120° but lower (tetragonal) symmetry than the regular cubic (10, 3) net. There is also a second net (6, 4), the NbO net (Fig. 128(f)) with equal coplanar bonds and bond angles of 90°.

The symbol (n, p) does not distinguish between, for example, the two 3-connected nets (10, 3), which represent different ways of joining 3-connected points into three-dimensional systems of 10-gons. The two nets are not inter-convertible without breaking and rejoining links. Not only does the most symmetrical configuration of one net possess higher symmetry (axes and planes) than the most symmetrical configuration of the other, but the *topological symmetry* of the former is higher than that of the latter. Unlike the crystallographic symmetry the topological symmetry does not involve reference to metrical properties of the nets, but only to the way in which the various polygonal circuits are related one to another. Two quantities that may be used as a measure of the topological symmetry of regular nets are: x, the number of n-gons (here 10-gons) to which each *point* belongs, and y, the number of n-gons to which each *link* belongs. For a plane net x is equal to p, the connectedness, and y is always 2. In 3D nets x and y can attain quite high values, and for the very symmetrical nets of Table 18 y is equal to n. For these nets x and y are related: $x = py/2$, an expression that holds for the (3, 4)-connected net if weighted mean values of x and p are used. In the second 3-connected net (ThSi$_2$) there are two kinds of non-equivalent link, and the weighted mean value of y is $6\frac{2}{3}$, as compared with 10 in the regular (10, 3) net. For the second 4-connected net mentioned above (NbO) $y = 4$. The values of x and y are not of interest from the chemical standpoint, but their determination from a model ensures that the model is examined in some detail and not merely assembled and dismantled.

A linked pair of 4-connected points, having 6 free links, is equivalent topologically to one 6-connected point, and a linked pair of 3-connected points is equivalent to one 4-connected point. It is therefore possible, by pro-gressive substitution of pairs of points (with appropriate values of p) for single points, to derive the 4-connected nets we have been discussing from the primitive cubic lattice and the (3, 4)- and 3-connected nets from the diamond net, provided the interbond angles and/or the dihedral angles have suitable values. This way of deriving them is used in building models of certain of the nets in this book.

Further 4-connected 3D nets

Of the indefinitely large number of more complex nets we have illustrated the wurtzite (tridymite) and PtS nets in Fig. 5(c) and (d), p. 13. The 'Fedorov' net, in which the links enclose truncated octahedral cavities, is the simplest 4-connected member of the group of polyhedral frameworks; it has been illustrated in Fig. 6 (p. 14).

Radiating 3-dimensional nets

In a p-connected system there are $\frac{1}{2}p(p-1)$ ways of selecting two of the p links. Considering the p links from any given point in pairs we can find the smallest circuit that includes both links of each pair. We may recognize as a special family (uniform nets) those in which the shortest circuit is an n-gon for each of the $\frac{1}{2}p(p-1)$ pairs of links and give them symbols n^3, n^6, etc. for 3-, 4-, etc. connected nets, the 'indices' being the values of $\frac{1}{2}p(p-1)$.

For 3-connected systems the tetrahedron (3^3), cube (4^3), and pentagonal dodecahedron (5^3) conform to this definition, and the next member (6^3) is the plane hexagon net. Two ways of realizing higher members of the series have already been noted, namely, plane radiating nets (for any value of $n > 6$) and 3D nets (up to 10^3). Examples of the last group are the 3-connected 10-gon

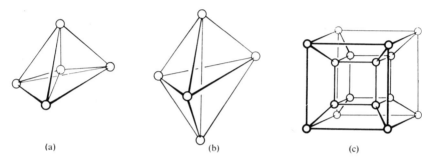

(a)   (b)   (c)

FIG. 129. The 4-connected systems 3^6 and 4^6 (see text).

nets described on p. 171; the intermediate nets 7^3, 8^3, and 9^3, have also been derived. (For 3-connected nets either symbol, n^3 or n, 3, may be used.) A third family of nets $(n, 3)$ is mentioned in the next section.

The 4-connected systems are rather more interesting. For $n = 3$ the system consists of a central point connected to the vertices of a tetrahedron, or the topologically equivalent case where the central point is projected through the base of the tetrahedron to form a bipyramid (Fig. 129(a) and (b)). For $n = 4$ each vertex of a cube is connected to one of the vertices of a circumscribing cube (Fig. 129(c)). In contrast to the finite 3^6 and 4^6 the system 5^6 is an infinite radiating net which starts from a central pentagonal dodecahedron (Fig. 130). This is surrounded by a shell of twelve dodecahedra which is succeeded by further shells of dodecahedra. This radiating 5^6 is the net R_4 of Table 19. The radiating 6^6 is found to be identical with the diamond net, i.e it is also periodic in three dimensions. There is also a radiating $(3, 4)$-connected net with 6-gon circuits which occupies the position marked $R_{3,4}$ in Table 19.

This table summarizes the simpler 2- and 3-dimensional nets and includes a number of polyhedra. One of the five regular solids, the 5-connected icosahedron, is omitted because there are no corresponding networks in two or three dimensions which fit into the simple scheme of Table 19. On the other hand, two semi-regular polyhedra, the trigonal bipyramid and the rhombic dodecahedron (with both 3- and 4-connected vertices), are included because they are clearly members of both the horizontal and vertical families.

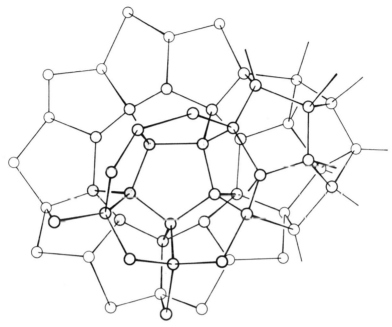

FIG. 130. The radiating 4-connected system 5^6.

Infinite polyhedra

We have seen that there are definite upper limits to the values of n and p in systems (n, p). To simplify our discussion we consider triangulated tessellations $(3, p)$. The upper limit is $p = 5$ for a convex polyhedron and $p = 6$ for the Euclidean plane. Topologically the vertices of the regular solids may be regarded as sets of points symmetrically arranged on a sphere, a surface having (constant) positive curvature, and the regular tessellation $(3, 6)$ is possible on a surface of zero curvature. Tessellations $(3, p)$ having $p > 6$ can be drawn on a surface of constant negative curvature, but these hyperbolic tessellations cannot be realized in ordinary space. We have also seen that plane radiating nets $(3, p)$ may be drawn with no upper limit to the value of p. It may be of interest to the mathematically inclined reader that there is a family of surfaces on which tessellations $(3, p)$ may be drawn, apparently up to the limit $(3, 12)$.

If we imagine that the links of a net (2- or 3-dimensional) are 'inflated' so that they become tubes, or tunnels, meeting at the points of the original net, there result infinite periodic surfaces (of varying curvature). The number (t) of tunnels meeting at each point is equal to the connectedness of the original net; we retain p as the connectedness of the tessellation drawn on the surface. It is found that the equations relating to these tessellations are similar to equations (1)–(3) on p. 157 for polyhedra except that the right-hand side is now $2p(2-t)$ instead of $4p$. The equations for finite convex polyhedra are not meaningful if $p > 6$ because all coefficients of f_n are negative. However, the equations for these new surfaces do have solutions for $p > 6$. For example,

$$\text{7-connected:} \quad -f_3 - 6f_4 - 11f_5 - 16f_6 - \ldots = 14(2-t).$$

p / n	3	3 and 4	4	6
3	Tetrahedron	Trigonal bipyramid	Octahedron	Plane (3,6)
4	Cube	Rhombic dodecahedron	Plane (4,4)	P lattice ①
5	Pentagonal dodecahedron	Plane $(5,4)$	R_4	
6	Plane (6,3)	$R_{3,4}$	Diamond ②	
7	(7,3)	$(7,4)$		
8	(8,3)	$(8,4)$ ③		
9	(9,3)	$(9,4)$	$\textcircled{Z}$	
10	Cubic (10,3) ④			

TABLE 19. *Relation between polyhedra, plane, and 3-dimensional nets*

Such an equation has positive solutions for $t \geqslant 3$ and gives the required relation between the numbers and types of polygons forming tessellations on these surfaces. The numerical values of f_n (and of the numbers of points and links) are those corresponding to one repeat unit of the infinite pattern. For example, on the surface of the 'three-dimensional polyhedron' resulting from inflation of the links of the diamond net it is possible to draw (3, 7), (3, 8), and (3, 9). When drawn as tessellations on the surfaces of the tunnels the polygons have curved edges, but it is found that some of these 3D polyhedra may be constructed with plane equilateral polygonal faces. The triangulated polyhedra (3, 7), (3, 8) (two), (3, 9) (two), (3, 10), and (3, 12) are obviously the 3D analogues of the three triangulated Platonic solids, (3 ,3), (3, 4), and (3, 5).

Appendix 4

THE SYMMETRY OF CRYSTALS

Point symmetry: the thirty-two crystal classes

THE symmetry of a finite object is described by its *point symmetry*, which is a group of symmetry operations. These operations are of two kinds, axes of rotation (n) and axes of rotatory inversion ($\bar{n}$), and because the object is finite all the symmetry elements necessarily pass through a point. The possession of an axis of simple rotation (n) implies that the appearance of the object is unchanged after rotation through $360°/n$, n being an integer. An axis of rotatory inversion ($\bar{n}$) involves rotation through $360°/n$ together with simultaneous inversion about a point on the axis *as part of the same operation*.

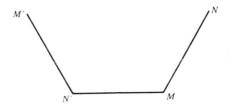

FIG. 131. Possible types of symmetry axis in crystals (see text).

The rotatory inversion axes include the familiar centre of symmetry ($\bar{1}$) and the (reflexion) plane of symmetry ($\bar{2}$), also written *m*.

There is no restriction on the value of n for finite objects in general; for example, a right pentagonal prism possesses a 5-fold axis and the molecule of $S_4N_4H_4$ an $\bar{8}$ axis. However, there is a very definite limitation on the types of axial symmetry that can occur in crystals, and this limitation also applies to the shapes of crystals, which are an expression of their regular internal structure. The atomic structure of a crystal is a periodic 3D pattern of atoms in which the only possible types of axial symmetry are 1-, 2-, 3-, 4-, and 6-fold. It is sufficient to show that this restriction applies to a periodic 2D pattern, which represents a plane section through the 3D pattern perpendicular to the axes in question.

In Fig. 131 let there be an axis of n-fold rotation perpendicular to the plane at N and at M one of the nearest other axes of n-fold rotation. Rotation through $360°/n$ about M transforms N into N', and the same kind of rotation about N' transforms M into M'. It may happen that N and M' coincide, in

TABLE 20. *The thirty-two classes of crystal symmetry*

Hermann–Mauguin	Schoenflies
Triclinic	
1	C_1
$\bar{1}$	C_i, S_2
Monoclinic	
2	C_2
m	C_s, C_{1h}
2/m	C_{2h}
Orthorhombic	
222	D_2, V
mm2	C_{2v}
mmm	D_{2h}, V_h
Tetragonal	
4	C_4
$\bar{4}$	S_4
4/m	C_{4h}
422	D_4
4mm	C_{4v}
$\bar{4}2m$	D_{2d}, V_d
4/mmm	D_{4h}
Trigonal	
3	C_3
$\bar{3}$	C_{3i}, S_6
32	D_3
3m	C_{3v}
$\bar{3}m$	D_{3d}
Hexagonal	
6	C_6
$\bar{6}$	C_{3h}
6/m	C_{6h}
622	D_6
6mm	C_{6v}
$\bar{6}m2$	D_{3h}
6/mmm	D_{6h}
Cubic	
23	T
m3	T_h
432	O
$\bar{4}3m$	T_d
m3m	O_h

which case $n = 6$. In all other cases NM' must be greater than, or equal to, NM (since M was chosen as one of the nearest axes), i.e. $n \leqslant 4$. The permissible values of n are therefore 1, 2, 3, 4, and 6. Study of the combinations of these axes n and $\bar{n}$ shows that there are only thirty-two possible crystallographic point-groups or classes of crystal symmetry (Table 20). For example, only the following types of hexagonal symmetry (i.e. having a single axis of 6-fold symmetry) are possible:

$$6, \ 6/m, \ 6m, \ 62, \ 6/mmm, \quad \text{and} \quad \bar{6}, \ \bar{6}m.$$

(The symbol $6/m$, a convenient way of printing $\dfrac{6}{m}$ (6 over m), indicates that there is a plane of symmetry perpendicular to the 6-fold axis, $6m$ that there

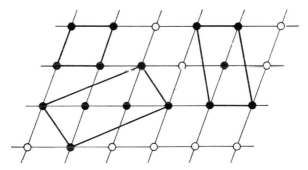

FIG. 132. Unit cells of 2D pattern containing 1, 2, and 3 points.

is a plane parallel to the axis, and 62 that there is a 2-fold axis perpendicular to the main axis. The symbol $6/mmm$ means $\dfrac{6}{m}\,mm$, one plane being perpendicular and the other two parallel to the 6-fold axis.) The thirty-two crystal classes are grouped into seven crystal systems as shown in Table 20, which lists the Hermann–Mauguin symbols used by crystallographers and the Schoenflies symbols often used by spectroscopists.

Since the internal (atomic) structure of a crystal is a 3D periodic pattern it can be referred to a system of axes along each of which the pattern repeats, at intervals a, b, and c. Together with the angles between the axes these repeat distances define a *unit cell* which is a parallelepiped containing a representative portion of the structure. Repetition of the unit cell in the three axial directions reproduces the (infinite) crystal structure. Consideration of a simple periodic 2D pattern shows (Fig. 132) that it is possible to choose a unit cell in an infinite number of ways, and the same is true of a 3D pattern. It is conventional to select a cell so that the directions of its edges are related to the symmetry elements (if any) of the structure. For example, one of the axes of a tetragonal crystal (*c* axis) is taken parallel to the 4-fold axis, while a crystal with cubic symmetry is referred to equal orthogonal axes equally inclined to the 3-fold axes, which are parallel to the body-diagonals of the cubic unit cell. The cell chosen in this way is not necessarily the smallest possible cell, as already noted in the case of the diamond structure (p. 170). The parameters defining the unit cells in the various crystal systems are listed in Table 21, which also includes the characteristic symmetries of each system.

TABLE 21. *The crystal systems: unit cells and characteristic symmetry*

System	Relations between edges and angles of unit cell	Lengths and angles to be specified	Characteristic symmetry
Triclinic	$a \neq b \neq c$ $\alpha \neq \beta \neq \gamma \neq 90°$	a, b, c α, β, γ	1-fold (identity or inversion) symmetry only
Monoclinic	$a \neq b \neq c$ $\alpha = \gamma = 90° \neq \beta$	a, b, c β	2-fold axis (2 or $\bar{2}$) in one direction only (*y* axis)
Orthorhombic	$a \neq b \neq c$ $\alpha = \beta = \gamma = 90°$	a, b, c	2-fold axes in three mutually perpendicular directions
Tetragonal	$a = b \neq c$ $\alpha = \beta = \gamma = 90°$	a, c	4-fold axis along *z* axis only
Trigonal†	$a = b \neq c$	} a, c	3-fold axis along *z* axis only
Hexagonal	$\alpha = \beta = 90°$ $\gamma = 120°$		6-fold axis along *z* axis only
Cubic	$a = b = c$ $\alpha = \beta = \gamma = 90°$	a	Four 3-fold axes each inclined at 54°44′ to cell axes (i.e. parallel to body-diagonals of unit cell)

† Certain trigonal crystals may also be referred to rhombohedral axes, the unit cell being a rhombohedron defined by cell edge *a* and interaxial angle α ($\neq 90°$).

The symmetry of 3D patterns: the 230 space-groups

In order to describe the symmetry of the internal structure of a crystal it is necessary to introduce, in addition to rotation and rotatory inversion axes, symmetry elements that involve *translation*, namely, screw axes and glide planes. A screw axis combines rotation around an axis with translation in the direction of the axis, and leads to a helical array of points, as shown in Fig. 23(a) (p. 44) for the operation of a 4_1 axis. For a 4_1 axis the translation associated with each rotation of 90° is $c/4$, where c is the pitch of the helix (or repeat distance along the 4_1 axis). In order to ensure that a point repeats regularly at intervals of c along the direction of the axis it is not necessary that the translation is $c/4$; it could have two or three times this value, the corresponding symbols being 4_2 and 4_3. A convenient way of showing the sets of points generated by screw axes is to represent them by sets of figures giving the heights of the points above the plane of the paper as multiples of $c/4$:

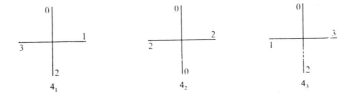

Starting in each case at the top of the diagram and proceeding clockwise, each point rises $c/4$, $2c/4$, or $3c/4$ for each 90° of rotation. A point at height $4+z$ is a point at height z in the next repeat period, but since by definition each repeat period must contain the same arrangement of points, this implies a point at height z in the original repeat period. Evidently 4_1 and 4_3 axes are

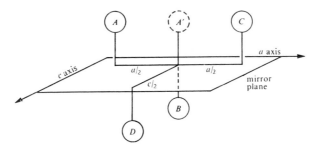

FIG. 133. The operation of a glide plane.

enantiomorphic pairs corresponding to clockwise and anticlockwise rotation, as also are 3_1 and 3_2, 6_1 and 6_5, or 6_2 and 6_4. The complete set of screw axes is:

$$2_1, 3_1, \text{ and } 3_2, \quad 4_1, 4_2, \text{ and } 4_3, \quad 6_1, 6_2, 6_3, 6_4, \text{ and } 6_5.$$

A glide plane combines in one operation a reflexion and a simultaneous translation. If we imagine a point A (Fig. 133) on one side of a mirror moved first to A' and then reflected through the plane of the mirror to B, then we say that A is converted into B by the operation of the glide plane. The same operation performed on B would bring it to C, the translation being always a constant amount $\frac{1}{2}a$, where a is the unit translation of the lattice. A more complex type of glide plane could transform A into D, this involving translations of $\frac{1}{2}a + \frac{1}{2}c$, followed by reflexion. If the unit translations a and c of the crystal lattice are not equivalent we clearly have three types of glide plane involving translations of $\frac{1}{2}a$, $\frac{1}{2}c$, and $\frac{1}{2}a + \frac{1}{2}c$.

The possible types of symmetry of periodic 3D patterns represent all the permissible combinations of the four kinds of symmetry element, simple and rotatory inversion axes, screw axes, and glide planes, with the various frameworks (lattices) on which the patterns are based. Instead of the thirty-two point groups which suffice to describe the external shapes of crystals, a total of 230 space-groups are required to describe the symmetries of their internal structures.

Subject Index

Formula Index

Ag[C(CN)$_3$], 10
(Ag$_2$I$_3$)Cs, 83
Ag$_2$O, 80

AlBr$_3$, 56, 82
AlCl$_3$, 82, 147
α-Al$_2$O$_3$, 63, 64, 109
AlOCl, 82, 141
Al(OH)$_3$, 147
α-AlO.OH, 99
γ-AlO.OH, 99
Al$_2$(OH)$_2$Si$_4$O$_{10}$, 155
Al$_2$(OH)$_4$Si$_2$O$_5$, 155

As, 16, 43
As$_2$O$_3$, 16
As$_2$S$_3$, 16

BN, 41

(B$_3$O$_5$)Cs, 124
(B$_4$O$_7$)Li$_2$, 124
(B$_5$O$_8$)Cs, 124

BaMnO$_3$, 69
BaNiO$_3$, 67
BaTiO$_3$, 109, 146

BeO, 85

Bi, 43
(BiF$_4$)NH$_4$, 33
BiF$_5$, 145
BiI$_3$, 60

C (diamond), 18, 44
   (graphite), 16, 41

CaAl$_2$Si$_2$O$_8$, 139
CaF$_2$, 74
CaTa$_2$O$_6$, 107, 153
CaTiO$_3$, 146
CaTi$_2$O$_4$, 116, 152, 155
CaV$_2$O$_4$, 151

CdCl$_2$, 60, 132, 134, 147
(CdCl$_3$)NH$_4$, 147
CdI$_2$, 60, 147
γ-Cd(OH)$_2$, 109

Cl$_2$O$_7$, 77

CoF$_3$, 61
CoMoO$_4$, 153

CrCl$_3$, 60, 132
CrF$_5$, 145
(Cr$_2$O$_7$)Rb$_2$, 77
CrPO$_4$, 155

CsCl, 128
CsNiCl$_3$, 67

(Cu$_2$Cl$_3$)Cs, 83
CuO, 51
Cu$_2$O, 80, 125
Cu$_2$(OH)$_3$Cl, 99, 150

FeCl$_3$, 82
FeF$_3$, 61
FeOCl, 99

GaOCl, 141

(GeF$_6$)K$_2$, 69
GeS, 43

(HgCl$_4$)K$_2$.H$_2$O, 147
HgI$_2$, 59, 139

KNbO$_3$, 146

Li$_2$O, 58
LiOH, 84, 141

Mg$_3$(OH)$_2$Si$_4$O$_{10}$, 155
Mg$_3$(OH)$_4$Si$_2$O$_5$, 155
[Mg$_2$(OH)$_3$(H$_2$O)$_3$]Cl.H$_2$O, 147
MgSO$_4$, 155
MgZn$_2$, 140

MnMo$_9$O$_{32}$$^{6-}$, 88
MnSO$_4$, 155

MoF$_5$, 145
MoOF$_4$, 145
MoO$_3$, 153
(Mo$_2$O$_7$)Na$_2$, 154